Helle Amin was born in De[...] teacher before moving to En[...] the UK she has studied acupunctur[...] of alternative therapies. Helle married in 1[...] traumatic experience, she has helped to support other women who have not yet been reunited with their abducted children. Helle now lives with her four boys in the West Country.

———————

Co-author David Meikle was born in Edinburgh in 1954. He began his career in newspapers, before moving into television. He is a former News Editor with ITV, and recently produced the ITV 50 series for the South of England. He has also produced and directed programmes for Meridian Broadcasting in Southampton. David now runs his own creative writing company, Clever Writing (www.cleverwriting.co.uk).

HELLE AMIN

REUNITED
IN THE
DESERT

HOW I RISKED EVERYTHING TO
SEE MY CHILDREN AGAIN

JOHN BLAKE

Published by John Blake Publishing Ltd,
3 Bramber Court, 2 Bramber Road,
London W14 9PB, England

www.blake.co.uk

First published in paperback in 2008

ISBN: 978-1-84454-606-0

British Library Cataloguing in Publication Data

A catalogue record for this book is available from the British Library.

Printed in Great Britain by Creative Print and Design, Blaina, Wales

1 3 5 7 9 10 8 6 4 2

© Text copyright Helle Ahnin, David Meikle 2007

All pictures from the author's collection except p.1; p.7, top right
and p.8 bottom right © UPPA

Papers used by John Blake Publishing are natural, recyclable products
made from wood grown in sustainable forests. The manufacturing
processes conform to the environmental regulations of the country
of origin.

Every attempt has been made to contact the relevant copyright-holders,
but some were unobtainable. We would be grateful if the appropriate
people could contact us.

This book is dedicated to my children, Max, Alex, Zak and Adam, who deserve to know the truth.

I also dedicate the book to my late father, Edmund; my beautiful mother, Grethe, who always believed in me; and all my family and friends.

My thoughts are with Nadia and Kauser, who at the time of writing are still anxiously awaiting news about their children. Their haunting stories deserve their place in this book.

I dedicate the book to all left-behind mothers and their children in the hope that they, too, can be reunited.

ACKNOWLEDGEMENTS

Dozens of people helped me, in so many different ways, in my campaign to reclaim my children.

First, I'd like to thank Professor Caroline Thomas of Southampton University. I couldn't have done it without her friendship and continued support. Caroline has been my solid, reliable rock.

I also received valuable help and support from: Abdullah Al-Johani, Ann Thomas, Chadi Zayout, David Meikle, Denise Carter, Hani Al-Malki, Henriette Karno, HRH Prince Turki Al-Faisal, Janet Sawyer, John Leggett, William John Neil, Kathy Kent, Maya Steinberg, Mr Matook, Mrs Fatin, Nattalia Sinclaire, Professor Steve Thomas, Richard Spalding, Roshra Mutain, Steven Martin Clark, Tracey Howard and Victor Mehra.

My heartfelt gratitude goes to the following people, who provided me with moral support, pep talks and constructive criticism during the writing of this book: Chris Alphey, Ebbe

Iskau, Graham Whitehorn, Michelle Clark, Karin Ladefogde and the rest of my 'Danish family' in England, John Lister, Jason Paterson, Judith Paterson, Shirley Sargent and Wilma D'Silva.

CONTENTS

FOREWORD
A Woman in
Two Worlds

I've spent the past few years travelling between two worlds. One world I was familiar with; as for the other, I still haven't got my head around it. In my familiar Western surroundings I prided myself on being a loving mum and a faithful, giving wife. In the new, harsh and cruel environment I was accused of being an unworthy Western woman, not fit to be a mother or a wife.

I've always been drawn to other cultures and I've travelled a lot, so maybe I was destined to find a husband with a background completely different from mine. I even converted to Islam, as I thought it would improve our relationship and make things easier for everyone.

I wanted to be happily married, with a bright future and kids running about my home. I thought I had the husband I wanted. I certainly had the kids I wanted, but I could never have predicted the ordeal that awaited me in the deserts of Saudi Arabia.

Nor could anything have prepared me for what was to happen in such a short space of time. I can only compare it to being brought up in, say, South America and then having to live the rest of your life at the North Pole. And I'm not joking.

I remember people telling me that I may as well give up, as it was virtually impossible to get into Saudi; that my quest to find my children and gain custody of them was a non-starter. I could see why my advisers and even some of my friends were so negative.

And, after researching the subject of child abductions, I myself realised that the success rate for mothers trying to regain their children wasn't high. I talked to dozens of organisations, lawyers and mums who'd lost their children and took on board all the advice I could get.

When I weighed up the facts, my task looked uphill all the way. All the mothers I talked to had endured traumatic experiences; many had fought a lone battle to get their children back; most told me they felt dead inside; several were going through financial hardship. Only very few had managed to be reunited with their children.

After my experience of free-and-easy British culture and then the laidback lifestyle of Bali, I was about to enter another, totally unfamiliar world. I took for granted what it was like to stretch out on a beach and sunbathe, go out for a glass or two of wine or enjoy a night at the cinema. This new world didn't have much of any of that.

I was used to getting behind the wheel of my car and driving, without having to think about it. I enjoyed walking along the road, completely free, with the wind blowing in my hair. Awaiting me in this other world were religious police who were determined that not even a strand should show.

I was a Western girl used to a Western lifestyle. I'd long enjoyed all the thrills and frills, and that's the only way of life I knew. But looming on the horizon was a desert, barren geographically and spiritually, where I could never ever fit in.

When I put my case before a Saudi court, I realised I was a bit of a one-off. So rare was it for a Western woman to be standing there outlining her case that all the men present seemed to look uncomfortable. No matter how much you try, if you're not born a Muslim you'll never convince them that you and your views have any value.

Every day in Saudi Arabia, I felt as if I was no one at all, walking around with most of my body hidden from view. A Saudi woman has little status; but a woman from the West has *no* status. Why hadn't I married again? There must be something wrong with her if she hasn't married again. I could sense that's what Arab men were thinking. They simply thought I was too unworthy to even give me the time of day.

Despite that cool welcome in the desert, I was prepared to do anything to get my children back. I flew thousands of miles and begged every favour I could from anyone and everyone.

I was told I had to have a relationship just to obtain the correct paperwork. Now that's something I would never have contemplated; but when it's a case of 'children or no children', a mother has little choice. I was a desperate woman, prepared to take desperate steps. Now, after doing just that, I look around me and see my four boys laughing and joking once again.

What you are about to read involves sadness, humour, human strengths and weaknesses. There are high points and some exceptionally low ones as I find myself on a rollercoaster that just keeps on going.

I felt qualified to write it. I married a Muslim; I became a Muslim myself; I lost my children; I had to live in Saudi Arabia and pursue justice through both the Saudi legal system and that of my own world. The whole process has left me a wiser and stronger person. Inevitably perhaps, I've also become much harder.

Along the way I've made fantastic friends, people who rallied to my cause and would do anything to help. I met others who fiercely opposed what I was doing; as for them, we'll just have to stay worlds apart.

PROLOGUE

I stood on the stage at the Waldorf Hilton Hotel in London, wondering if this was really happening to me. Mum of the Year? Surely this sort of thing happens to other women, not me?

That evening in January 2006 I saw so many famous people. The radio DJ Matthew Wright introduced me and told how I'd been chosen by *Tesco Magazine* as Mum of the Year in the Best Children's Entry category. A video showing me and my boys all together at our new home in Devon played on an enormous screen.

From the stage, through all the lights, I could just make out happy faces, dazzling white tablecloths and exotic flowers.

Matthew quoted from a letter written by my eldest son, Max, who'd nominated me without letting me in on the secret. Matthew said the Tesco judges had been moved by what they read. I overflowed with pride as I stood on the stage and he read an excerpt from Max's letter:

'Something happened to us in 2002. My father, who's from Saudi Arabia, took me and my brothers away to live there. It was really, really hard for us as we'd never been to the country before.

'It was a very different place to live, and we didn't speak the language. Worst of all, we'd never been apart from our mum and we really, really missed her.

'Mum spent 16 months trying to find out exactly where we were. Then she faced a long, hard battle with the Saudi Embassy to get a visa to see us out there.

'When she eventually got to Saudi Arabia, she got a job at an international school so she could be near to us and she fought in the courts to get access to see us. We were allowed to visit her for 24 hours a week.'

So many thoughts flowed through my mind as I stood there. Cameras flashed. Max squeezed my hand. I gave his hand a quick squeeze back, then tried to compose myself.

I could see my friends in the audience clapping. In a few seconds, I went through such a range of emotions: happy, sad, jubilant, tearful, excited, proud.

Matthew told my story and then asked me a few questions. I hadn't prepared anything but when I answered I just went into full flow and it all seemed to come naturally.

I received my award as loud music played and my sons smothered me with hugs. Denise Carter, director of the charity Reunite, who has supported me through everything, presented me with a stunning bunch of flowers and an engraved crystal vase. In a powerful speech, Denise said my story was an inspiration to other women in my situation.

Why did Max send that touching letter to *Tesco Magazine*? You're about to find out.

1
STOLEN

The twenty-third of January 2002 started like any other day on my tropical island. Warm sunshine, growing hotter by the minute, filled my room and it was time to get up. I woke the children and went downstairs to discuss the day's schedule with our two maids. One of them had already made breakfast.

'It's ready,' I announced, hoping the household might pay attention. 'It's on the table,' I added after a few minutes in a slightly louder voice, hoping for more success.

The boys arrived from their bedrooms in a hurry and grabbed bread and jam from the table before heading for the television room.

'Sit,' I insisted and they screwed up their faces in disappointment. 'No TV this morning, it's a school day.'

'But, Mum, please ... please ...' five-year-old Adam pleaded.

'No way. Sit nicely at the table.'

The twins, Max and Alex, also raised their objections.

Typical ten-year-olds, they had a growing list of favourite shows on satellite. Zak, although two years younger, was up to speed on all the episodes.

Any thoughts of television were wiped off the menu when T arrived for breakfast. He looked to be in the blackest of black moods. The table fell silent. At least the kids are eating their food, I thought. I didn't realise it was to be our last breakfast together for 16 months.

'I'll take them to school,' said T, as usual delivering no more than the basic facts. 'We're leaving now. See you later.'

The kids collected their bags, kissed me and followed T out of the front door. His car engine started, the doors closed and my children were gone.

I stayed in my chair for a while. I needed to work out how to improve the atmosphere in the house. I had to think of a way of easing the strain in my marriage.

We should never have left England, I told myself as the maids busied themselves around me, piling up the boys' plates. Why on earth did we ever set up home in Bali?

I cast my mind back over my recent past, picking out the major problems and analysing them. The move to Bali had seemed a good idea at the time. T had set up a furniture business on the island and, despite its spectacular failure, we had stayed on and converted the building into The English School Bali.

To start with, it was an exciting project and I felt it would work, using my experience as a qualified teacher. It soon became obvious that T and I couldn't work together. After putting in a lot of hard graft, I was now back to being an obedient housewife.

The maids left the room, but I stayed in my chair, still

trying to work everything out in my mind. Why do I have to obey his every command? I asked myself, at the same time knowing that I'd always have to obey. T ruled the house with his filthy moods and I despised his tantrums. How I hated them.

Looking back, big trouble must have been looming on the horizon for some time before the children vanished. We bickered and we argued, but didn't most couples do that at times? I was trying to reassure myself. But reality kicked in. This was spiralling out of control.

'I hate my life, I hate my life,' I kept repeating.

The maids could see that I was miserable, but they had no idea what I was saying.

I finished the rest of my cold coffee and went up to my bedroom – I no longer shared a bed with T – for another thinking session. Maybe it didn't help that I was a feisty type, I wondered. Perhaps our personalities clashed. Surely I should have a say in the running of the school, as I'd played a major role in setting it up? Why didn't he want my input?

I lay on the bed and probed deeper into our disastrous relationship. In my head I compiled a list of grievances. For a start, I had to ask for money if I wanted to buy shopping for the household. I didn't ask for any expensive luxuries as I knew that they would be out of the question. T kept everything under his control. He even had the children's passports hidden somewhere. I was trapped.

I tried to go back to sleep. There was little else for me to do as the maids took care of the household chores. A holiday island is ideal for holidaymakers, but if you live there it soon loses its attraction.

My attempt to get more sleep failed dismally. I wanted to

talk to someone, but my close friends and family were on the other side of the planet.

As the day wore on, like so many before, morning drifted into lunchtime, then into afternoon. I just went with the flow, like a piece of driftwood floating off in no particular direction.

T and the children came home from school about three o'clock on what would turn out to be the worst day of my life by quite a margin. T had a quick cup of tea, provided by one of the maids. We didn't exchange a word, or even a glance, and he went out again. It was as if I didn't exist in his world any longer.

The children played, just like any other afternoon in Bali, and then finished some homework. The first hint of the imminent nightmare came in the form of a phone call that afternoon. It was from one of the British teachers at the school. 'You'll never guess who I've just seen at Immigration,' said the nervous voice, slowly and deliberately. 'T was there, and he seemed to be collecting passports, and I think exit visas for your children and him. I couldn't see exactly, but he seemed to be getting those passports, so I thought I'd better tell you.'

My friend knew about our marital problems, and so naturally she wondered what was going on at Immigration. She said she'd overheard T talking to an official there. I knew that business people had to apply for exit visas if they wanted to leave Bali. It's different for tourists.

I asked her to repeat what she'd seen, and as she did so I felt a shiver running through my body from top to bottom. My stomach churned and I felt sick. At the same time, I felt angry and tense. The pain was both mental and physical. I fought my emotions and managed to stay calm.

When T returned at dinnertime, I asked him to sit down and talk. He refused, saying he was busy. I persisted and followed him around the house.

'Why did you take the passports to Immigration? What's all this about exit visas? Where are you going? What the hell's going on?'

He didn't have an exit visa for me. I knew this because my passport was still in my handbag.

When I told T what my friend had said, he became very aggressive. He insisted it was perfectly normal to obtain exit visas in case they had to leave the island; it was just a routine paper exercise. I could see that I was being fobbed off.

From the look on his face it was obvious that he'd been taken completely by surprise. He looked as if he'd been clobbered by a sledgehammer. He was bright red and looked totally stunned. I had obviously caught him out big time, but he still wasn't going to tell me what was going on.

It was time for T to scarper. Before I could ask him any more questions, he ran out of the house. I could hear him saying something about an important meeting. The words 'passports' and 'exit visas' filled my head. Surely he couldn't be planning a holiday without me, or was something even more sinister on the cards?

I ran after him and shouted, 'I demand an answer now. Come back here and answer my questions.' I was surprised at how assertive I sounded, and for a few seconds I was pleased with my firm stance.

I tried to run in front of him, but he pushed me out of the way. He shut the gate firmly behind him. Before I could catch up with him, he was in his car and off up the road. I remember breaking down into floods of tears in the middle of the road because, whatever was going on, I certainly wasn't supposed to be part of it.

While T was out having his 'meeting', I put the children to bed, kissed them and tucked them in – the last physical affection they were to receive from me for nearly a year and a half. The last boy I kissed was Zak. I gave him a tender peck on the forehead and left the room.

Then I carried on with my normal chores and helped the maids to tidy the house. After that, I decided to stock up on some essentials at the local shop. I needed bits and pieces to put in the boys' lunchboxes for the next day.

I was out for 40 minutes at most. While I was shopping, I wondered if I should have left the house at all. I thought about keeping an eye on the boys 24/7, but dismissed the idea as impractical. A pre-emptive strike, taking them to a friend, would have been more sensible, but I didn't think of that at the time.

Driving home, I had a growing premonition that something wasn't right. As I approached the house, I was gripped by terror. Call it a mother's instinct, call it what you will, I knew deep down inside that something terrible had happened.

As I pulled up outside the house, one of the maids ran towards me. 'They've gone,' she blurted out in broken English. 'They've gone.'

I raced inside like a woman possessed. As I tore through all the bedrooms, I was sobbing and desperate. I wanted my children so badly. Where were they? Had my worst fears come true? I shouted at the maid at the top of my voice: why hadn't she called my mobile?

She started to cry and I felt awful. She worked for T as well as me, so she must have been totally confused. I tried to get her to explain what had happened. Her English was far from perfect but I understood that, as soon as I left to go to the shop, T had come back and woken the children.

She said T had told the boys to get dressed but Alex didn't want to put his shoes on. That made sense, because he has a strong character and would have held out as long as possible. Perhaps, I thought, Alex was stalling for time until I returned. But, when T shouted at him to hurry up and get in the car, my boy would have stood little chance of resisting, even though he knew something was wrong.

T had talked about taking the boys out for a soft drink and a snack, the maid said. They didn't seem to take much with them. All that was missing was a small orange bag. T wouldn't have fitted much in there. I relaxed for a moment, thinking he couldn't have gone far with the boys.

I was in an emotional state and desperate to find out what had happened to my family. But I had no idea where they were, if they were safe, who was looking after them – all the normal feelings that any mother would have. I went right through the house again, searching for the tiniest clue. I emptied drawers, thinking there may be some paperwork somewhere, but I found nothing. All I could detect in the house was negative energy; 100 per cent negative.

Outside, I checked around where the car had been parked. Maybe something had dropped out as they left. I looked up and down the road in the faint hope that I would see something. There was nothing. Thoughts of T and my children raced around in my head and I could feel a flood of tears running down my cheeks.

I jumped into my Espace and took off. That evening, I could have been in contention for the Renault Formula One team. I've never driven so fast. Apart from braking for the occasional bend, I kept my foot down all the way.

Following my instincts, I made for the school, about four miles away. I knew that many of our personal possessions were kept in the safe there, so it was a good place to start. As I sped along, I tried to call T's mobile. I'd have had more chance of reaching one of the Saudi princes on his day off. T's mobile was on voicemail. I left messages even though I knew I wouldn't be getting any replies.

When I reached the school, the confused-looking security man at the gate told me, with a combination of English and sign language, that T and the children had been and gone. I was on their trail, but losing ground rapidly.

What was I to do now? I ran, weeping, through the classrooms. I rang everyone I could think of. They all said I must be mistaken. T would never abduct the boys like that, they reassured me, but my instinct told me otherwise. Sick with worry, I drove on to a friend's house and tried to calm down.

Eventually, I decided all I could do was go back to our villa, in the hope that T had returned with the boys. No such luck. There was no sound of the front gate opening, or of my children's footsteps and voices.

It was past midnight when I lay down on the sofa, absolutely exhausted. I closed my eyes and pictured my boys, at the same time trying to get to grips with what had happened. I fell asleep but woke up in the early hours. As I jumped up, I realised I was still alone in the house.

I didn't want any more sleep and anyway I knew I had to make full use of every precious minute. I drove back to the school and resumed my search for clues. As I hunted through the classrooms, my mouth dried up and my entire body shook.

On the desk in the office, I found a letter addressed to me in T's handwriting. I must have missed it the first time. I ripped it open. T had written that he'd taken the boys away for a few days as he felt they needed to spend some 'quality time together with Dad'. He said he would call me the next day. In the envelope with the letter was US$100.

I waited at the school until about eight o'clock, when the secretary normally arrived. She opened the safe for me, and a quick glance inside confirmed my suspicions. Cash, papers and my jewellery had vanished. It was like watching one of those movies where a gang crack open a safe, expecting to get their hands on untold riches. And, just like them, I was confronted with emptiness.

I called an Australian lawyer friend who lived in Bali to ask for advice. I knew T had his passport, the boys' passports, exit visas, other important papers, bank books and cash. My friend suggested I should go to the airport and check passenger lists on all flights leaving the island. I bribed a clerk at the information desk to show me the list for the next eight hours, but I couldn't see T's or the boys' names anywhere.

By this time, it was one o'clock in the afternoon and the boys had been missing for 16 hours. I'd spent nearly every minute of that time searching for them, and it felt like 16 months.

I returned to the school for a third time. The first thing I saw was T's car. Thank God, he'd brought the boys back! I ran inside the school, my heart beating loudly. I didn't find

T or my children there. Instead, I found a rather puzzled Indonesian with T's car keys in his hand.

It turned out that T had left his car in Denpasar, the capital of Bali, earlier that morning and paid someone to bring it to the school in the afternoon. I wasn't going to have the children but I could have custody of a Japanese 4x4, was T's message.

At this point, of course, I had no idea where they'd gone. All I knew was that the car was back at the school. I prayed that they were still in Bali, but I knew they could be anywhere. I'd never wish that sense of helplessness on any mother. I felt like screaming, climbing up the wall, tearing out my hair or doing anything that would express my utter despair.

I drove home. I didn't know where to turn, who to speak to or how I could relieve my misery.

The children's clothes and washing were still at the villa. Toys, school bags, everything was there. The smell of the children was there still. Their lunchboxes, waiting to be filled, were still in the kitchen. It was like a ghost house. In my head I could hear their voices, but they were gone. Would I ever see them again?

I was growing ever more desperate. The police didn't want to know. My lawyer friend tried to call them on my behalf, but they weren't interested. I was a foreigner with foreign kids. Why should they care?

I contacted the British Consulate, but the staff there didn't want to know either. They just said they couldn't help me, and suggested that I should contact the police. I'd tried that and there was nothing doing.

Back at the school, lessons were still going on and there was a sense of normality, although naturally everyone kept asking, where's T? Where are the children? I was hoping that he would just show up with them. I knew I had to act normally too. But by now I wasn't eating or sleeping and I found it difficult to concentrate on anything except the disappearance of my sons and how I was going to find them.

The next day, I felt as if I was in a dead zone. I just ran around in circles, getting nowhere. I phoned everyone I could think of who might know what had happened.

I called my teacher friend Linda, who worked in another school in Bali, and she came over to stay with me. I was losing track of the days. T and the boys had vanished on Friday and it was now Sunday.

With Linda I went over everything, trying to put all the pieces together. I thought long and hard about the events leading up to my nightmare. I told Linda that T had sent a letter to my family in Denmark a week before taking the boys. He had written to them that I was anorexic, in a bad psychological state, and that it would be far better for all concerned – including the boys – if I went back there on my own.

He said I wasn't a fit mother any more and I had really changed. I wasn't good to him or the boys and the time had come for me to leave Bali. He added that he would be really happy for anyone in the family to come and get me and he would contribute to the air fare.

It was true that I had lost a lot of weight, but it was because of the pressure of our troubled marriage and feeling I had to cope with everything day to day on my own. Worry and anxiety had built up in my mind over the weeks leading up to the boys' abduction, so I'm sure I did look very different from my normal self.

Linda pondered over my plight. A thoughtful woman, she arrived at carefully worked-out conclusions before speaking. She told me what I had suspected, but the truth pierced my very being like a dagger.

'He wanted you to leave the island on your own,' she said. 'He wanted to get rid of you. He wanted to make you so miserable that you'd just leave. He was trying to break you.'

I gasped, then wept uncontrollably. Linda tried to stop me crying, but I couldn't stop.

'His plan didn't work out,' she whispered, her arm around my shoulder. 'He obviously had a plan B. It's worked for him but it's almost destroying you.'

She decided to stay overnight and after we'd shared a bottle of wine we dozed off on the living-room sofas. I tossed and turned for a few hours until I woke with a start. It was five o'clock. Who could be ringing so early in the morning? The voice on the other end of the line was instantly recognisable.

'Where the hell are you? Where are the children?' I demanded. I knew I didn't sound very calm. My fear, distress and anger all came out at once.

'Listen to me, Helle,' T said. 'I'm at my brother's house in Jeddah, in Saudi Arabia. The children are here, next to me. We've left Bali for good and we're now living here.'

The truth was grim, and difficult to get my head around. T and the boys hadn't flown out of Bali. He had left the car at the garage, caught a taxi to the bus station and from there my boys had endured a 22-hour non-stop journey by bus and ferry to Jakarta, the Indonesian capital. How could anyone take four children, the youngest only five, on a dangerous trip like that?

12

'The children are excited and they are happy,' T went on. 'They're with their cousins, having a great time. We've started a new life. As we entered Saudi Arabia, I handed in the children's British passports. The children are now Saudi citizens and we will live here for ever.'

Those words haunt me to this day. I can still hear him saying 'for ever'. As he said it, I saw vivid images of my children and tried to imagine what it would be like never to see them again. It was the most awful thought.

At first I said I didn't believe him. Jeddah in Saudi Arabia? Then I asked to speak to his brother, to get him to confirm my worst fears. The boys' uncle, Adnan, had always seemed quite reasonable, and I guessed he knew how I was feeling.

Adnan said the boys were indeed in Saudi. He sounded uncomfortable and quickly passed the phone to them.

'Hi, Mum, we're having a great time,' the twins said at once and I could hear them jostling for position. 'We're having a nice holiday.'

'We're playing with our cousins and they've got some cool toys,' Zak yelled above the commotion around him. 'Can't wait to see you.'

'Love you, Mum,' was all Adam said.

I wondered if things could get any worse. My children had been abducted, but they thought they were on holiday. They were waiting for me to arrive.

T loved to be in charge; I'd known this from the time I met him. In England, he'd always liked to be the boss and he'd wanted to be the main man in Bali too. Despite this, or perhaps because of it, both his business and his marriage had now failed.

Teachers and parents at the school found him difficult to

work with and said he was 'too controlling'. Perhaps he'd felt that he was losing control there as well.

Now he was in Saudi with our children. I could tell from his tone that he was feeling in charge again. He was making the decisions. In his eyes I was a very poor second in the relationship, or what had at one time been a relationship.

His stance confirmed that I had a nightmare of a task ahead. He was holding all the right cards, including a fistful of aces. I was stunned. As I tried to see through a haze of tears the truth hit me hard.

Even as we talked I could see my future mapped out in front of me. I'd read somewhere about fathers taking their children away to Saudi and other Muslim countries. Well, now it had happened to me. My life was shattered. I pledged then that I would devote my life to finding my boys. I vowed that we would be reunited in the desert.

'T, what the fuck have you done? You bring my children back – now!' I hissed.

T was back in charge. He hung up.

2

ALONE

I gaped at the telephone in disbelief for several minutes, as Linda sat silently beside me. I cried and she cried for me. I couldn't speak. Then Linda's tears stopped and the expression on her face changed.

'You're going to have to pull yourself together right now,' she said sternly, looking straight into my eyes. 'This isn't the time to break down. Your children are out there in the desert and you're going to find a way of getting them back.'

I was shocked. It felt as if Linda was lecturing me.

'You'll have to fight this battle alone,' she warned me as she opened the curtains on a new dawn I didn't want to see. 'The children need you more than ever. If anyone can get into Saudi and rescue those kids, it's you.'

I phoned my mum in Denmark to share my grief. She called the rest of my family and they all rang me. Everyone was devastated by the news.

Over the next few days, every time I hit a low I thought

of Linda's words. I also kept going over and over the appalling conversation I'd had with T. I wondered when and how he would tell the boys that Mummy wasn't coming, after all.

For all Linda's words of reassurance, I felt completely numb. I couldn't stop trembling and crying; I just felt so helpless. Every time I thought about my children I had pains in my stomach. Still unable to sleep or eat, and looking tired, drawn, thin, just terrible, I decided I couldn't go on living like a shell of my former self. I had to keep going for my children's sake.

Linda left my villa at about eight that morning to go to work. Her words were still ringing in my ears as I prepared a 'to do' list. There was so much I had to do. I went for a long walk to think through my master plan.

As the news about T started to filter out into the community, things became really difficult. Parents of pupils at the school were worried about their children's education. I assured everyone that I'd do my best to keep the business going, but I could see a cash-flow crisis looming.

Linda kept calling to check that I was all right. 'How on earth anyone could do this to another human being is beyond me,' she said several times.

I looked around to see what could be done. We'd just taken delivery of six new computers. I sold them back to where they came from, at a loss of course, but I needed to put money back into the school. Next I sold our two cars and hired a small tired, old 4x4. It looked as if it had come from an army surplus store. The brakes worked after a few seconds and it backfired a lot, but it went from A to B and usually back again.

My extensive list of problems kept on growing. I discovered I'd been working illegally in Bali. T had never obtained a work permit for me. I reckon he just didn't want to pay for one. He said that because my degree was from Denmark I wouldn't qualify for one anyway. This was obviously a load of nonsense and within a few days I was legal again.

Uppermost in my mind, though, was the fact that my children were no longer around me. When parents asked me what was going on, I told them the truth.

To my horror, I found out later that one of the teachers had helped T with his escape plan. It was a woman I didn't get on with. I hadn't trusted her from the moment I met her and I knew she didn't like me much either. She knew what T was up to and helped him to formulate his escape. When I found out through various sources, I sacked her on the spot.

I organised a staff meeting to restructure the running of the school. I told the other teachers what they knew already: T and the boys had gone and now I was in charge. The teacher who had spotted T at Immigration became my second-in-command.

I tried to reassure everyone that we could keep going. We held a parents' evening, where mums and dads wondered what would happen to the fees they had paid. They had also handed over cash for school trips and events, so they wanted answers quickly.

I was a woman under pressure. The tax people found problems with the bookkeeping. They wanted an awful lot of money and I couldn't pay them, so I sold off more equipment and paid someone I knew to sort it all out. The less said about that the better.

Linda had been 100 per cent correct: I would have to fight my battle alone, and I hadn't even started to tackle the issue of my children yet. Linda was the only person I could trust with everything. I made a key decision and decided I should call her with the news.

'I'm going to sell up,' I told her, trying to sound upbeat. 'It's the only way out. Everyone's on my case. Please keep up your support because there are a lot of two-faced people at the school.'

I shared some of my problems with another friend, Nattalia, an elegant and kind Englishwoman who was married to a Balinese businessman. I also shared my thoughts with George, a handsome South African who proved to be a loyal friend. More about that relationship later.

I knew that another school on the island had been interested in my business; I was competition, after all. I thought I'd approach them before I went crazy. They made me a reasonable offer and I took it. My only condition was that all the staff would be kept on, and the buyers were true to their word. They also made sure that the parents weren't out of pocket.

I knew it was the right move, because by now I was dealing with a procession of people saying they were owed money. Anyway, I just wanted to concentrate on tracking down my sons.

Next I pondered what I should do about the villa. I couldn't live there, because of all the memories it held of the children. I could only spend a short time each day at home sorting things out before I just had to get away.

It was evident now that T and the children weren't returning to Bali. I called Uncle Adnan's house almost every day, as I knew that was where they were staying. I had very little money, but what I had I spent on those calls.

Nothing had changed. Adnan allowed me to talk to the kids, who were clearly expecting me to join them. T told me that he'd send them to school and reminded me in no uncertain terms that they would be staying in Saudi for good. I wondered how long he would wait before telling them that I wasn't going to be part of the set-up.

He said he wanted the boys to grow up with their cousins and to be brought up as Muslims. When I told him I would fight him on all fronts until my dying day, he laughed.

A letter arrived for me and I recognised the handwriting at once. It was from T. The first page was a handwritten letter saying that he had divorced me in Saudi Arabia. The second page was a photocopy of the divorce certificate in Arabic. Ironically, the divorce helped me in my quest. Getting into Saudi as a married woman would have proved a harder task, as he would still have been 'in charge' of me.

Through some speedy research on the internet, I discovered that in Saudi Arabia a man can divorce his wife at any time. He doesn't need a reason and it doesn't matter what his wife has to say. By contrast, a woman can't divorce her husband unless she can prove he's been unfaithful – and three witnesses are needed.

One evening Nattalia phoned to check if I was all right. She was just the tonic I needed.

'You're in no state to live there,' she said in a warm, soothing voice. 'Why don't you come and stay with my family?'

'I'm fine,' I lied. 'Honestly, I'm fine and I can cope, but thanks so much for offering.'

She knew I was putting on a brave face. I called her back

and admitted that I was having a disastrous time. No, I wasn't coping well at all, and yes please, I'd love to stay with her.

I packed a bag and within half an hour I was knocking on her door. Nattalia cared for me and helped to keep my emotions in check for three months. With Linda and George also checking on me, I was in good hands.

The villa, as I mentioned before, was a big problem. Eighteen months earlier, in one of his impulsive moments, T had rented a piece of land on a 20-year lease. It was cheap and right next to the main road. An endless stream of motorbikes and cars passed by, en route to the beach.

One side of the plot bordered a school playground, the back bordered a pig farm and the other side was home to an extended family of chickens. During the rainy season, the smell from the pigs took over.

It must have been one of the worst-sited foreign 'villas' in Bali. The rainy season hadn't figured at all in the planning process. T designed the house with an Indonesian architect who'd never built to a high standard. To keep the cost down, he used the cheapest materials available. As usual, I didn't have a say in the project.

I was desperate to sell the villa, or even rent it out, but I couldn't get anyone interested. It was lovely inside, but the flaws in the construction work were only too obvious. The busy road outside wasn't an attraction either.

Bali is one of the most spiritual places I've ever known, so I wasn't entirely surprised to have a strange experience while I was trying to sell the house. You could say everything turned sweet and sour. I'd shown a potential buyer around the villa and, as we were leaving, I closed the front door behind me; I felt something was wrong and went back into the garden. Two trees – a sweet mango and a sour mango – had stood there for many decades. Maybe they sensed the grief all around; they were dead.

After that, I turned my attention towards getting out of Bali as soon as possible. I knew that the urgent help I needed awaited me in England. I made plans to visit the Foreign Office, the Saudi Embassy, solicitors and bodies such as Reunite. Thoughts of help on the horizon kept me going. My faith in all these organisations stopped me from breaking into a thousand pieces. I believed that, as soon as I returned to England, everyone would help me and my case would be sorted. It didn't quite turn out like that.

T had made a clever move in taking the children away from Indonesia. He knew the British courts wouldn't be able to help me, and I quickly realised that the Indonesian legal system was a waste of time.

I became concerned about the constant pain in my stomach, which I put down to worrying and missing the kids. Many months later, when we were reunited, the pain vanished.

I did all I could to keep in touch with the children. I phoned them almost daily. For that I have Uncle Adnan's wife, Alia, to thank. She insisted that I should talk to the boys whenever I called. I sent them parcels every week containing small presents, clothes, letters and photos. I asked their friends in Bali to write to them regularly. I guessed correctly that sooner or later contact would be lost.

I explored all possible means of getting to Saudi Arabia. I knew many Indonesian Muslims went on pilgrimages there. During these trips, Muslims visit all the holy places of Islam.

As I didn't have the required Muslim father, brother or uncle to escort me, an organised tour seemed to be the answer. I would still need to be looked after by a licensed maharam, a male Muslim sponsor. I would have to stay with the group all the time and perform the religious duties of a Muslim.

It became clear to me that going to Saudi as part of an organised tour wouldn't provide many opportunities to see my children. So I was still stuck in Bali, and still thinking.

Many people have asked me how I managed to stay sane and not 'lose the plot' during this very confusing and emotional time. The answer is that, whenever I felt myself slipping down the slope of depression, I closed my eyes and imagined my four little boys standing in front of me. I could picture them looking up at me with their beautiful, big brown eyes, saying, 'Hey, Mum, we need you.' I just took a deep breath and got on with it.

But a couple of incidents did nearly push me right off the rails. One busy morning I was driving through Kuta, near Nattalia's house, in my rented apology for a vehicle. I stopped at a T-junction and then carefully inched out on to the road. A gang of young boys on motorbikes appeared from nowhere and didn't stop, and one of them went straight into my front bumper. The boy flew through the air and landed on the road.

I can still hear the crunch of the metal. Shit! I pulled over to the opposite side of the road, where I could park safely. I looked in the rear-view mirror and saw that the boy was still lying on the ground. The other boys in the gang, presumably thinking I was about to do a 'runner', came over to my car shouting and screaming. In no time, a crowd of local people gathered to see what had happened.

Thank God, the car was locked, as the boys tried to open

the doors. They were banging on the car and shouting in Indonesian. I didn't dare get out and try to calm them. I had to think fast. I took my mobile phone out of my bag and called an Indonesian male friend, Djati.

I was so lucky that he was out on his motorbike near by. While I was on the phone, an older Indonesian man from the growing throng kept the gang away from my car. He asked me to roll down my window. I quickly explained in broken Indonesian that my friend would be arriving shortly.

The man said that the boy's leg was injured. I could see in the mirror that the lad was sitting up and talking, so I felt relieved. He was alive.

Djati arrived and quickly got things organised. He carried the injured boy to the front seat of my car. I climbed in the back, and Djati drove to the nearest hospital, in Denpasar. We were followed by a convoy of at least ten motorbikes.

Anyone familiar with a state-run hospital in a Third World country knows that it's not a pretty sight. When the doctor eventually sees you, he makes a list of things he needs to 'mend' you back together. A relative or other person – in this case, me – goes to the hospital shop and buys what is needed. It's then all brought back to the doctor.

The boy's leg was broken in several places, so the doctor put it in plaster and I paid the hospital bill. Now, remember, I didn't believe that the accident was my fault. However, I was a foreigner in a car. The boy was Balinese. I was in no position to put up an argument. The last thing I needed was a group of unhappy males from the boy's extended family turning up on my doorstep.

I agreed to pay for a rented car to take the boy to his village on the other side of the island. On top, I had to pay for the repairs to his motorbike. There was no point making an insurance claim, as it's an expensive and complicated business in Bali.

A week later, three of the boy's relatives did turn up at the school. They demanded money for the check-ups, plus six months' lost wages. Their calculation of what they thought was reasonable would cover private treatment in the UK. It took an entire morning for the school secretary, Djati and the family members to come to an agreement.

So I owed an awful lot to Djati. As well as rescuing me from the motorbike incident, he actually saved my life. In fact, thinking back, he was always there for me. Djati was an architect and had helped to design our house, but I won't hold that against him! He did help me out of several tricky situations, so I'll always be indebted to him.

All those unhappy episodes made me even more determined that it was time to leave. I had no desire to go through any more upsets in Bali. I just wanted to spend my time and energy finding a way to see my children.

One night I was invited for a dinner party at a friend's place in Ubud, a town in the middle of the island, about an hour's drive from Kuta. It was the first time I'd driven there on my own. I have always been rather hopeless with directions and I drove around Ubud for quite a while trying to find my friend Victor's house.

After dinner and a chat about my catastrophic life, I decided it was time to leave. When I reached the end of his drive, I couldn't remember whether I was supposed to turn left or right. I was too stubborn and too proud to turn back and ask for directions. I was feeling rather upset. My friends at the dinner all knew my sad situation and we'd discussed it for a good part of the evening. I missed my children so much and everyone there had tried their best to comfort me.

After a minute's tussle with myself, I turned left. I put on a tape of my favourite music and drove through one Balinese village and past one rice paddy after another. It was very dark and the villages all looked the same. But I was sure I was on the way home. Then it suddenly occurred to me that I wasn't going downhill to Kuta, which is by the sea. The road was getting smaller and heading uphill. I didn't recognise it at all. It was about one in the morning and I went into full panic mode.

Oh my God, I was on the road to the north of the island, driving through the mountains. Bandit country.

Occasionally I'd encounter a motorbike or car, but I couldn't ask for directions: I was too afraid to stop. I looked at the cars carefully, hoping to find a stray tourist, but no such luck. I felt vulnerable.

Several miles up the mountain road, after some sharp, dangerous corners, I found a place to turn the car round. It was outside a village cafe, where the local male population were hanging out. They looked a frightening bunch. I managed to turn round and zoomed down that steep, winding road at breakneck speed.

Crying hysterically now, I felt the loneliest I'd ever felt. Like some crazy woman, I started chanting my children's names. At last, I ended up passing my friend's house and pressed on to Kuta.

I reached Nattalia's place in an exhausted state. I went straight to bed but was too shaken up to sleep. I was completely drained of energy. My conclusion: it was definitely time to leave Bali.

During my quest, I met many people who helped me to be reunited with my children. Hani is one person who stands out. He's a Saudi businessman who has a large company and property in Bali. He was introduced to me by a mutual friend. At our first meeting, in an exclusive beach restaurant, he listened to my unhappy story.

'Please can you help me?' I asked.

He produced his mobile phone and called the one person he believed could help me – his mother in Jeddah – and she gave me the name of a lawyer who'd supported many women in my situation.

This key figure who took up the challenge on my behalf was called Abdullah. Hani's mother told me about his legal skills and I liked what I heard. She also told me that he had an English wife.

I was nervous about talking to Abdullah, but when I plucked up the courage to call him in Saudi Arabia he was friendly, understanding and helpful.

He did, however, stress that he couldn't do much for me until I returned to England. He made it perfectly clear that a Western woman, planning a trip to Saudi alone, needed more than a little help from above.

'There are some things I must ask you. Are you sure you don't want to go back to your husband? Can you not retrieve your marriage?'

'Absolutely no way,' I said, 'but with your help perhaps I can retrieve my children.'

The reason he'd asked about possible reconciliation was that, in Islamic societies, Sharia law requires everyone involved in a marital dispute, including relatives and friends, to try everything to patch things up. Divorce is a last resort.

I shared my news about the lawyer with Nattalia, who made sure I kept up my positive outlook. She decided I also needed a faith-healing session, so she introduced me to John.

John went through all my problems with me, healing what he could with crystals and stones. He asked me about the villa and reckoned it also needed some treatment from him.

We met a few days later and I showed him my former family home. He walked around and got a feel for the place. His verdict was that there was stagnant, negative energy that needed to be moved. The next morning we met again at the house. This time I was armed with my favourite music and dressed in work clothes.

An ugly bamboo screen in the garden was the first casualty. I'd always hated it.

'Take that, and that,' I yelled as I aimed several kicks at the screen. It disintegrated. I was sweating and swearing, letting all my anger flood out.

After going round the garden, we looked into every room in the house. Any item identified as negative by John was under sentence. Even the garden shed wasn't spared the wrath of this feisty Danish blonde. Anything that wouldn't burn was left outside for the rubbish collectors.

The new positive vibes in the property worked wonders. Three days later, a couple came along and rented the house. First stage of mission completed: school and house sorted.

I booked my one-way ticket to London. I was about to leave behind the tropical island that had held so much promise of happiness for me and my little family. When I boarded the plane, I was overwhelmed with sadness and loneliness. As we took off, tears were streaming down my face.

I left Bali on 6 October 2002. At that time, there was a real sense of prosperity and well-being on the island, with tourists arriving in droves. Blinded by my hopeless marriage, I hadn't appreciated it.

Perhaps someone above was looking after me. Six days after I left, the Bali bomb exploded. It was so shocking, especially as I passed that nightclub several times during a normal day.

I knew several of the people who died. One of my friends who perished was a beautiful girl in her twenties, half-German and half-Indian. I just couldn't believe that she'd been killed. She had a gorgeous two-year-old daughter.

Of course, what had happened to me paled into insignificance when I read about the bomb and how the economy and everything went downhill after the blast.

I'll say a lot more about my life in Bali later. I'll tell you about the island's unique traditions and customs. I'll tell you how the place nearly drove me mad. And how I found love there. But I can see now that I was fortunate to get out of the place alive.

3

CRIES FROM THE DESERT

I knew that Alex, Max, Adam and Zak would seek out the truth eventually. I was allowed to talk to them on the phone, thanks again to Alia. When that contact stopped, the boys tried to find ways of getting in touch with me.

I guessed – and I was right – that they'd be told what a bad mum I was. They were very young, but old enough to know that all I'd done was to smother them with love during our precious years together. Why was I such an awful person now?

They started to write letters and poems. Some they managed to send to me when I was in Bali; some found their way to England; and the others they kept until we were reunited. Adam must have spent a lot of his time drawing houses and trees. I believe that, because his mind was in such turmoil, those little works of art provided a welcome distraction and gave him a sense of security.

I laughed when I read: 'You make me smile when I feel crummy. There is nothing like you as my mummy.'

I cried when I read: 'I miss you every day when we are apart. Even when I do a fast.'

The letters filled me with hope because I knew that – whatever was being said about me – the children didn't believe a word. Have a look at what follows, and imagine the range of my emotions as I read their cries for help ...

We'd been back together some time before I asked my boys if they would like to help with this book. I explained to them that it would be interesting to hear the story from the real victims' point of view. I said the book was really about them and, after months of mulling things over, they agreed. It took a long time to get the information out of them, because it meant stirring up painful memories.

I'm sure that Zak could become a male model. He's so handsome. As it happens, he did some modelling in Bali for Australian catalogues. Now he's at school in Devon and, although his grades aren't brilliant, he's top of the class in drama. That took me by surprise because, when he was little, I thought he would excel at school. His horrific experience in Saudi put him off his studies. That may change; only time will tell.

Zak is the quietest of my boys. He has a temper, though, and a very strong character. I can read the twins and Adam like an open book, but not Zak. He keeps his emotions bottled up inside, until they come pouring out. When he snaps, he snaps badly and flies into a real rage.

The last boy I kissed before the abductions, Zak was also the first one I saw when I met them in an awful confined flat in Saudi.

If you remember, I was out shopping on the day my boys

were taken from our home in Bali on 23 January 2002. Zak says that while I was gone T came home and started shouting. He picked up an orange bag that he normally used for his sports gear. He barked orders to the kids and started putting clothes into the bag. It was around nine o'clock and they were already in bed.

Zak, who was coming up for nine at the time, recalls:

'I didn't really understand what was going on at first. Dad was storming around, asking where our mother was. The maid said she was out at a supermarket.

'He was yelling to us to get dressed and get ready. Alex was crying and said he wasn't going to put his shoes on. Dad continued shouting, forced on Alex's shoes and dragged him from the room. Our father isn't someone you argue with when he's upset; you learn to do as you're told.

'I started to get out of my night clothes and just put on some clothes from my cupboard quickly. I was still trying to understand what was going on as I was half asleep. Dad said he was taking us for a drink of juice.

'I remember thinking that it seemed odd to be going out for a drink late at night before a school day. I didn't have any choice but to go along with it, and wondered where he was taking us for our cola or orange juice. I could see that my brothers were also thinking what I was thinking. Dad hardly ever took us out, so what on earth was going on?

'Finally, after more shouting and crying, we clambered into the car, and Alex was still sobbing. We

were all asking why Mummy wasn't coming. We didn't hear an answer.

'Dad said we had to stop at the school, to get some money for drinks. He drove into the forecourt and ordered the security man to close the two large gates. I thought that was strange at the time. Well, everything seemed strange.

'Dad went inside the school and we waited for ages in the car. We were really sleepy, and I remember thinking that this was such an unusual outing. And we hadn't had our drink yet. I decided I'd have my favourite mango milkshake, and in my mind listed the places where we could be going.

'Dad reappeared with a big box and he put it in the back of the car. We wondered what was inside the box. My brother Max, who's a bit of a joker, thought there must be a lot of money inside so we would be getting lots of drinks.

'Dad got into the car, slammed the door and told us all to be quiet. He made sure the security guard closed the gates behind us, and we drove off. We seemed to drive for a long time, it was very hot and we didn't go for a drink.

'Instead, we pulled up outside a small-looking hotel. It had a swimming pool, so we all thought at once that we could have a swim. I thought, How nice, we can enjoy a drink and a swim. No such luck. We were all hustled up into a room and ordered to bed.

'There were two single beds. The twins, Max and Alex, shared one of the beds. I got into the other bed, with four-year-old Adam, who obviously didn't have a clue what was going on. He was just tired.

'Max, Alex and I started complaining. Why were we in a hotel? Why hadn't we had our drink? Where was our Mummy? Dad seemed very angry, upset and busy. We thought we'd better keep quiet. One of the hotel staff knocked at the door and I heard Dad saying to him not to tell anyone we were staying there. I saw him give the porter something; maybe it was money.

'By this time it would have been about eleven o'clock. We all started to get very tired, and we were due to go to school the next day. Our orders, though, were to stay quiet and go to sleep. We didn't dare to say anything, but I could see Dad sorting through papers in the box he'd taken from the school. I could see money as well.

'There was another knock on the door and in came one of the teachers from the school. That was a surprise but, as I didn't know what was going on, Santa Claus or Mummy could have been the next to come in.

'Dad and the teacher sat for ages in the corner of the room and talked and talked. I couldn't hear or understand, really, what they were saying but when I peeped out from under the blankets I could see they were both looking very serious.

'I saw Dad giving the woman a bag, and that's all I remember from that night. I must have fallen asleep, because the handing over of the bag is my last memory. When I woke up, the first thing I saw was my dad sitting on a chair between the two beds, crying. Although I was only eight, I realised that something awful was going on. I'd never seen my father crying before.

'He was saying he didn't want things to happen like this, and it wasn't his fault. I didn't know what he meant or why he was crying.

'I heard a knock at the door as I was waking up. It was the teacher's daughter. I knew her because I often saw her at the school. She would have been about 18 at the time, I think, and she was very nice. She was half-Balinese, and she used to stay with us and play with us. I couldn't work out why she had come, and we kept asking Dad about Mummy. We were just told to keep quiet.

'Dad said he had to go out and the girl would look after us. We said we'd all like a swim, but Dad said we weren't allowed to go in the pool. We had to stay in the room and the back garden of the hotel until he returned. He said he was going out to buy us some nice new clothes.

'We just played until Dad came back, and he did have lots of bags of clothes and shoes for us. We were told to have showers and get changed into our new clothes. I remember Dad putting lots of things into a big suitcase; maybe he bought that at the shops too.

'We got all packed up and ready to go. We climbed into the car and drove around for a while before arriving at what seemed to be a garage. We got out of the car and Dad gave the keys to the man at the garage. I remember clearly Dad giving money to the man at the garage and then hailing a taxi. We drove for a long time in the taxi, and then came to a place where there were buses. Dad had tickets in his hand and was looking upset. His face was looking all screwed up and serious.

'We got out of the taxi and had to walk close to him,

34

holding hands. As we got on to the bus, we had to find seats as it was crowded. We sat for what seemed a long time before the bus started moving. We were all very confused at what was going on, but thought we had better trust our father.

'As the bus started moving, Dad turned around from his seat and started talking to us. He said we had to listen to what he had to say, very carefully. As I remember, he said that life in Bali had become really miserable and sad, and he wanted us to have a good life, and everything would be wonderful.

'He wasn't going to tell us where we were heading for, but he reassured us that we were going somewhere nice and wonderful. He said we would be very happy there. He said that, for sure, Mummy would come and join us soon and we would all be happy there.

'We stopped several times along the way for snacks and drinks, and I was told later that the journey by bus and ferry took 22 hours. I only knew it was a place called Jakarta because that's what Dad told us. It could have been anywhere, but I knew it was a long way from my mummy.

'We stayed in another hotel in Jakarta for two nights, I think, and then we flew to Singapore. Dad went to the Saudi Embassy there to have our Saudi passports renewed because the old ones had run out.

'From Singapore I remember we had a stopover – I think it was Bahrain – and then on to Saudi Arabia. We didn't know we were going to Saudi until we were out of Indonesia. He kept saying we would have a fantastic new life.

'When we asked about Mummy, Dad said we could go back on the next plane if we wanted, but we would have a miserable life. We'd miss out on all the fun in our new home. Not to worry, he said, Mummy would be coming over to join us soon. We would be diving in the Red Sea, playing with our cousins and enjoying yummy food. Dad was starting to say that Mum was bad and horrible and wasn't a good wife or mother, but she would be coming to join us. It was all very confusing because later he would say she was just coming to visit. I now know that the plan was for her not to come at all.

'I remember getting out of the plane in the dark in Jeddah and it felt so hot. I just remember feeling hot and confused, and wondering, What is this place? We were greeted by Uncle Adnan at the airport; I'd met him when I was very young, but didn't remember him.

'He drove us to his house, and there we were greeted by his wife, Alia, and two maids. I didn't really know who was who, because they were covered up. I later learned that Alia had to cover up because my dad was not a blood relative; I discovered you have to cover up in front of men that you could marry.

'Once inside, we met our four cousins – two girls and two boys – for the first time and it was very exciting. The maids had prepared lots of traditional Arab food, and it tasted really nice. I think it was a meal of chicken, rice and salad.

'Dad explained to us that we would be living with his brother Uncle Adnan and Auntie Alia for a while until we found our own place. I can't remember exactly when, but, soon after we arrived, Dad called Mummy in Bali. He talked to her for a while, then Uncle Adnan also spoke to Mummy, and we were all called over to the phone.

'We were each allowed to talk to Mummy for a short while. We were having a really nice time with our cousins, and I asked Mummy when she was coming over to join us.

'I couldn't understand why Mummy was sounding so upset, and she seemed to be crying. She said she missed us and loved us, and would come to see us as soon as she could. I didn't know that wasn't going to happen. I didn't know I wasn't going to see my mummy for 16 months.

'We stayed with Uncle Adnan for a few weeks, and then we moved into a flat but we weren't very happy there. We didn't have the excitement of having our cousins around at Uncle Adnan's place. We didn't like the flat, because we were just there with Dad, we couldn't go outside because it was so hot, and the flat was beside a busy road.

'After what seemed a long time, Dad announced that we were going to school. My twin brothers and I went to a Saudi International School, which meant some Arabic lessons and some of the type we were used to, such as English and maths.

'I felt sorry for my little brother, Adam, because he had to go to a Saudi school where they only learned in Arabic. Adam only spoke English, like the rest of us, and it was very hard for him. He said the teachers and the other children weren't nice to him. Dad took Adam out of there, taught him at home for a bit and then put him into the same school as us.

'At some point, Dad said he was going to get married again. He introduced us to a woman who looked like Auntie Alia, and she seemed to be very nice.

'Dad rented a big house in Jeddah. It was like a ghost house. He used one of the rooms for his acupuncture clinic. My brothers and I slept in the same room in bunk beds. I remember Dad's new girlfriend coming over during the daytime, and one day Dad said they were getting married.

'She had a really nice family and we went over to see them a lot. They bought us lots of toys and clothes and they made us feel a bit happier. They did a lot to make us feel good.

'Dad seemed happier, too, and he was nicer to us. He and his new wife had their wedding in her family's house, and I know now that Dad had divorced Mum under Sharia law. He told us all that was what had happened.

'He also made a point of telling us that this was our new mum, and that was what we had to call her: "Mum". We didn't call her "Mummy", as that was what we called our real mother. When we first came to Saudi, we were told that we had to call our real mum "Helle". That was what we had to call her in our poems and letters.

'Everything seemed to be OK at first, and everyone got on well in the big house. We weren't allowed to talk to Mummy, and she mustn't have had our number because she didn't ring. I remember that after a while

Dad and his new wife began to argue. They were arguing about the same things as I remembered back in Bali. It was all about food and cleaning. We didn't have a maid, and I think the new wife was objecting to doing all the housework and cooking, all by herself.

'Dad got us all together and said that we were going to have a little sister or brother. The arguing did get a lot worse. One day after school, we came home to find that our new mum had packed all her stuff and was getting ready to move back in with her family. She was picked up by one of her relatives, and away she went.

'It was better when she was gone because, although she was nice, we were fed up of the arguing. She loved little Adam, and I got on fine with her. She wasn't so keen on the twins because they didn't like her telling them what to do. They said they didn't want to call her "Mum" because they already had a mother.

'We were really missing our real mummy, and after a few months in Saudi we weren't supposed to write any letters. We did write down some stuff, knowing that we had no way of posting anything. When Dad told us that we had to leave the house and move again, we were worried that Mummy might never find us.

'We imagined Mummy following a trail to where we'd been staying, and needing signs from us. We found a big piece of wood in the garden, and carved a message for her. We also wrote a special letter which we placed under the wood. We said that we were moving to the university compound, and we prayed that she would find the piece of wood with the carving and the letter.

'It was great living at the university compound. We were there because Uncle Adnan was a professor at the university, and he had a flat there that he wasn't using. We all stayed in the one room again, but we had a lot more fun because we met new friends and could play outside in the evenings.

'That was to be our new home, until we left Saudi Arabia. We had been in the country for a year, and never left the city of Jeddah. During all the three years we were in Saudi, we left Jeddah only twice, once for a trip to the mountains and once to Mecca. We hadn't done all those wonderful things we were promised.

'And we still hadn't seen our Mummy.'

4

ABOUT ME

Everything that's happened in my life has been out of the ordinary. I can't explain why, but it's been that way right from the beginning. All of my years have been filled with drama, excitement, tragedy, humour and a fair amount of hassle.

An unsuspecting world greeted me on 22 August 1964. My parents themselves were surprised that I was on the way. My 50-year-old dad and my mum, at 43, hadn't planned on extending their family. I already had two older sisters, Ingrid, who was 21 when I was born, and Sylle, who was 18 at the time, and a brother, Ole, who was 14.

When my mother was pregnant with me, she thought she was having an early menopause. She went to the doctor and was sent home with a suspected virus.

Well, it was no menopause and no virus either. It was me! My entry into the world was dramatic. My mum was taken to a small country hospital where there was only one doctor and a nurse on duty. Halfway through labour, the doctor realised a natural birth wasn't going to happen. He decided he'd have to act as the anaesthetist as well and carry out an emergency Caesarean section. The fact that I'm here today is a testament to his skills.

Almost from the minute I was born, I had three sets of parents. Ingrid's husband-to-be, Leif, was introduced to the family on my first birthday. Sylle's fiancé, Svend (pronounced Sven, but no football connection as far as I'm aware), was around from my birth. From my very early years, Svend came over to our house every night for dinner and was the only one who could get me to sleep. I even called Svend 'Dad' sometimes. When Svend and Sylle married, I had my own room in their house. So, as well as my real parents, I had other lovely people looking after me.

When I was four, Ingrid had her first son. Two years later, Sylle had her first daughter. I was six and remember everything so clearly. Rikke was born on my birthday, also by Caesarean. The doctors tried everything to get her out, and once again mother and daughter almost died.

I wasn't too keen on that little baby taking my place. Rikke was a beautiful little princess – and loved and adored – but I felt somehow that I was losing out. Looking back, that sounds awful but it's how I felt at the time. She was getting all the attention!

My first memory of my brother was when he arrived home from duty in the army. Ole joined up when he was 18, and I can picture him now arriving home on leave in his little red MG sports car. He looked rather dashing in his brown leather jacket. I loved being taken for a spin round the block. He was a handsome boy, so there was always a queue of attractive young ladies waiting for a trip in his car.

I grew up in a small village called Dianalund, about 70 miles west of Copenhagen. My father was a landscape gardener and a musician. He and my mother had a flower shop and a delicatessen, and, because the village was built around one of the biggest mental hospitals in the country, there was a lot of easy trade on our doorstep. The business really picked up around the time I was born.

My dad supplemented our income by playing saxophone, violin and piano at various events in the area. He told me how he'd survived during the war years and that the music had pulled the family through. My parents were married during the fighting and, because money was incredibly tight, my dad had to use some of the cash they'd received as wedding presents to pay for a taxi to the church.

Denmark was invaded on 9 April 1940 and our armed forces were defeated on the first day. My mum was working as a housekeeper in Copenhagen at the time. She could see the air base and recalls the German planes coming over and lots of explosions.

Most of the Danish merchant fleet escaped and sailed to Allied ports. Over the next four years, 60 per cent of these ships were sunk by the German Navy and around 600 Danish sailors were killed transporting Allied supplies.

Unlike other occupied countries, Denmark was able to retain its monarchy. The Danish government expelled Allied diplomats and imposed strict press censorship.

Denmark was forced to supply Germany with food and raw materials. This created problems for the Danish economy: the country suffered from inflation and the government had to impose food rationing.

Opposition to the German occupation grew in Denmark

and anti-Nazi newspapers began to appear. A resistance organisation helped thousands of Jews to escape to Sweden. Denmark was liberated by the Allies on 5 May 1945. My dad and one of the band members set up their equipment in the local village hall and played all day. It turned into an enormous celebration.

Times were hard and the only way my dad and his band could make a living was by learning tunes from the radio and performing them. They cycled about the countryside, sometimes for hours, with the instruments on the handlebars, on their way to gigs.

When I came along in 1964, my dad was still showing off his musical talents. He took in private students and still played around and about, although by this time a van had replaced the bikes as transport.

Because I was an unexpected arrival, I was spoiled rotten. I had everything I could possibly want. We lived above our flower shop and delicatessen. There was a large garden at the back but I often played with my friends in nearby woods. It was an idyllic lifestyle for a young child. My parents' business became successful and I enjoyed the rewards.

In those days, children didn't start school until the age of seven and I had marvellous playtimes with my little chums. I didn't learn to read or write until I was seven. That's just the way it was in Denmark then: families wanted their children to spend most of their early years having fun. Nowadays, Danish children start school at six years old, but attend only half of each day, so there's still plenty of time for play. Because they tend to work hard at school, they progress rapidly and by the age of ten they're up to speed with their English counterparts.

My main playmates, Anita and Helene, were older than me. They bullied me a little and if I played with them I often had to bring sweets from our shop.

My parents adored me. My dad never shouted at me or even told me off. To him I was a little princess and I remember being good most of the time. But I did get into trouble with my mum once. I used to walk a quarter of a mile to the village school with my friends. On the way home one day, Jorgen, one of my naughtier chums, decided we should explore his dad's sawmill. We played hide-and-seek in between all the dangerous equipment and massive logs, and we were having such fun that I completely forgot to go home.

Mum came looking for me, found me and dragged me home by the hand without saying a word. When we got back, she took me to the bathroom, pulled my pants down and gave me an almighty smack. That was the only time she ever smacked me, but I deserved it.

I was very fortunate to enjoy my first year of school. Fru (Mrs) Stissen taught everyone on her own and, because there was only one classroom, my year went to lessons in the morning from 8 till 12 and Year 2 were taught in the afternoon.

I'd been at the village school only a year when it was closed down and we were sent to what seemed to me an enormous school a few miles away. There, I was soon in for a reality check. I realised that my parents were so old: my dad was nearly 60, my mum 50, and they must have looked more like grandparents. It was a chance for other children at the school to tease me. 'How old is your dad?' they would ask, having a good laugh. Some of my friends' parents went to school with my sister!

45

My sisters and brother were much older than me, so I'd always felt that I was different. I grew up as an only child and from very early on I was aware of being surrounded by adults telling me what to do all the time. At times, I felt stifled. I was a strong-willed, independent child and I could feel myself beginning to rebel against my parents and all the other adults who were ruling my life. Those feelings of independence were starting to overwhelm me.

My parents' business was going well, which allowed them to take up travelling as a hobby. We went on the early charter flights to dozens of destinations, enjoying at least two holidays abroad every year. The seeds were sown then for my life of travel and love of other cultures.

Several of those holidays stick in my mind. We were among the first tourists to go to Morocco, which was so cheap at the time and yet so exotic. It was the mid-1970s and we stayed at the Hilton in Marrakesh. We explored the Atlas Mountains, bartered at the markets and soaked up the local lifestyle. I found it all so exciting. I had wanderlust, and that craving to find out about other cultures has been with me ever since.

I discovered England when I was 13. My father sent me to a language school in Worthing in West Sussex. I lived at 8 George V Avenue. Isn't it odd how details stick in your mind and stay with you for ever?

I attended the school twice during the summer holidays and studied English for six hours a day. About 25 children were sent from all over Denmark and we stayed with different families; mine were lovely. I remember thinking how odd it was to see English children going to school in their uniforms. In Denmark, I'd just worn casual clothes to school. I formed a strong bond with England and I knew I'd be back. I simply loved the people, enjoyed the countryside and was fascinated by our day trips. To me London was like heaven.

English food doesn't have a good reputation, but one taste was enough for me. I couldn't get enough English breakfasts or Sunday roasts. I was hooked and I'm addicted to proper chip-shop chips to this day. I still find it hard to walk past a chip shop; the aroma drives my taste buds wild.

My language studies in England complete, I returned to the school in Dianalund, where I took the equivalent of GCSEs and then went off to another school nearby to study for my A levels.

When it came to boys, Morten was my man from the age of 15. My parents liked Morten, whose father ran a local business. We enjoyed plenty of quality time. We often talked about sleeping together, but took a while to get round to it. He was two years older than me and I was exceptionally shy. One weekend we decided that the time had come.

I called my brother and suggested that, if it was all right with him, I would pretend to stay at his house for the night. Morten told his parents that he'd be staying with his brother at his flat. Of course, his brother wasn't there, so we had the flat to ourselves.

I felt innocent and naughty at the same time. I'd just turned 16 but it seemed that we'd been going out for ages. We knew each other really well and had gone through all the foreplay. It was also the first time for Morten.

It was a lovely, natural and gentle experience. I considered myself really lucky that it went so well. For the first few minutes, I did lie back and think of Denmark, because everything was so new to me. But, as our passion rose, I got into it more and more.

Morton and I saw each other for another two years, but we were exactly the same as most kids: new friends and ideas came along and we drifted apart.

By the time I'd finished my studies, I was well and truly sick of school. My wanderlust took over and I packed my bags and headed for Israel on my own. The usual way was to go with a group of five or six people, but that couldn't be organised for a few weeks and I didn't want to wait. Teenagers didn't normally take off to a kibbutz alone, but my mind was made up. My friend Kirsten said she'd follow on a month later after completing her studies.

So, off I went on the plane to Tel Aviv at the tender age of 18. I arrived on a Friday and I had to go to the kibbutz office in the middle of the city to collect my papers. When I reached the office, they told me I might be stuck in Tel Aviv for the entire weekend, as the following day was Shabbat. I knew that on this day of rest and spiritual enrichment everything would come to a standstill. Shabbat is a cornerstone of Judaism. It's the only ritual observance in the Ten Commandments: 'Remember the Sabbath Day to keep it holy.' Finding a bus to take me to the kibbutz, in the north of Israel, wasn't going to be easy.

A taxi rushed me to the bus station, where I saw the last bus until after the weekend pulling out. I waved frantically, running alongside it and doing my best to keep up. It was one of the oldest, most dilapidated buses I'd ever seen.

'Stop, please! Stop, please!' I yelled in vain as my only hope entered the traffic flow. It was going at no more than five miles an hour, so, although I was being covered in smoke from the exhaust pipe, I kept up a gentle trot, hauling my bags behind me. Seeing traffic lights approaching, I seized my chance. The bus stopped, the driver spotted me and happily took on board his new, bedraggled passenger. He also helped to pick up the contents of my bags, which had burst open from bouncing along the road.

After several hours of heat and extreme discomfort, the driver dropped me off at the end of a dusty track and I started to walk the rest of the way up to the kibbutz. I must have been spotted from the top of the hill, as an ancient tractor spluttered into life and lurched down the track towards me. 'Hi, I'm Hans,' the driver shouted above the engine noise. 'Welcome to the pleasure zone,' he continued in his broken English as I clambered aboard the trailer.

Hans must have been nearly seven feet tall. He'd arrived from Germany six months earlier. He had a shock of blond hair and a rugged, weather-beaten face. 'We do have a shower,' he reassured me as the tractor rattled back up the track and he looked at my filthy clothes and dusty, sooty face. Hans said he was leaving the next day and after he dropped me off I never saw him again.

For anyone who hasn't visited a kibbutz, it's a type of community where everyone is expected to contribute. Everyone puts the same in and everyone gets the same out. People come and go all the time. In this particular kibbutz, 800 people were permanent residents and there were 50 volunteers, including me.

I took to the lifestyle immediately, despite an unfortunate start. The people at the kibbutz weren't expecting me and there had been a mix-up with the paperwork. There were no spaces in any of the girls' rooms, so for a while I shared a room with two English guys. They were friendly and gave me enough space.

On my first night, I just crashed out. When I woke up, my two roommates had gone out to the fields to pick avocados. But I wasn't alone. Sitting on top of my unpacked bag was the biggest, hairiest, blackest spider I'd ever seen in my life. I hated spiders, but this monster was the daddy of all my nightmares. I was terrified. I made a slight movement; it flinched. I put my foot on the floor; it inched its way across the bag. Possibly it was harmless. I had no intention of hanging around to find out.

I saw my chance. The ugliest, most frightening spider in Israel crawled off the bag and, with an unexpected change of pace, darted underneath my bed. I jumped off the mattress, unlocked my door and ran for my life. The kibbutz leader and two volunteers gaped in astonishment as I raced past them. They had a good laugh when I described my predicament. The intrepid trio entered my room, stalked the beast and it was no more.

Our day started at four in the morning. One of those old tractors pulling a trailer took us up to the fields and we went to work. We picked grapes, cotton, avocados, bananas, oranges, melons, olives, tomatoes and dates as the sun rose and the Golan Heights shimmered in the distance.

I didn't speak a word of Danish for a whole month. Everyone spoke English, which was good for me, but I reverted to my own language when my friend eventually arrived.

I fell in love while I was working at the kibbutz. I'd had boyfriends before, but now I was desperately in love. In Denmark, I'd gone out with Morten for three years. Now, this experience in Israel was different. I met an English hairdresser, who also worked as a model. He had long, curly, blond hair and he was simply gorgeous. I don't think he was in love with me, though. Looking back, I think he was confused about his sexuality. We didn't go 'all the way'. It was just an innocent romantic affair with some snogging; he left, and that was that. However, he had a profound effect on me and it took some time to get over him.

For the first time in my life, I was putting on weight. I'd always been a skinny little thing. Now I was a stone overweight. We ate lots and didn't get enough exercise, and it all added up to those extra pounds. When I arrived in the kibbutz, I packed away a pair of trousers. A few months later, I tried them on and couldn't get them past my knees.

As well as working in the fields, I had a stint in the kitchen peeling potatoes. At the start of the day, a huge plastic container packed full of hundreds of potatoes looked a formidable sight. One of my fellow peelers was an elderly lady with a tattoo on her forearm. It looked like it had been there a long time and I just had to know what it was all about. The girl sitting next to me noticed that I was looking at the tattoo.

'She had it done during the war,' the girl whispered as we peeled together. 'The old lady doesn't talk about it. She didn't want to have the tattoo done; she was in a concentration camp during the war and the Nazis gave her a number.'

I ran from the kitchen sobbing aloud, and only the girl next to me knew what was wrong. I came back after a few minutes, gathered my thoughts and started peeling again, trying not to look at the old lady's tattoo or even to think about what she must have gone through at the hands of the Nazis.

My friend told me that she thought the lady was Polish. One day, she said, details about the concentration camp had emerged. The old woman had told her how prisoners were given serial numbers accompanied by shapes, symbols or letters. These identified the status, nationality or religion of the prisoner. I started to study the arms of some of the older kitchen workers. I could see more tattoos. I requested a transfer back to the fields; the kitchen made me feel too sad.

Kirsten and I left the kibbutz after about six months, as we had decided to go and explore Egypt. We took a bus from Tel Aviv to Cairo and did the full tourist bit. We took a train down the side of the Nile – a fantastic experience. We stayed in Luxor, hired bicycles, visited the Valley of the Kings and lived life to the full.

From Egypt, we travelled back to Israel before returning to Denmark.

Our next trip was Kirsten's suggestion. During our time at the kibbutz, she'd also fallen in love with an Englishman. No surprise, then, when she hinted at a stay in London. It didn't seem a bad idea, as Denmark was cold and miserable after the sunshine of the Middle East. Kirsten was desperate to see her man and I fancied checking out the English capital myself.

We took a ferry to Harwich and then the train to London. Having booked in at a YMCA hostel, we met another Danish girl, who was working as a maid in a five-star hotel. She said they were looking for more maids, so we turned up at the hotel the next day and were offered jobs immediately.

Yes, I fell in love again. This time it was with an Italian stallion, who also worked at the hotel. He was loud, attentive, charming, grumpy and sexy all in the one package. I remember eating a lot of pizza and spending time with his Italian friends, who were just as charming as he was.

I had my first encounter with Australians and soon I was a regular face at Aussie parties, where dozens of people packed into a small space and drank loads of lager.

My Italian returned to Italy, but by this time I'd had enough of him. He was very emotional, impulsive and had a real temper. Once, when his second-hand Rolex went wrong, he shouted so much at the shopkeeper that the whole street heard what was going on and turned up to gawp. I was so embarrassed I sneaked out of the shop and hid until he quietened down.

Scotland was our next port of call. We travelled around for a couple of weeks and looked up a Glaswegian friend we'd met at the kibbutz. What a culture shock. Glasgow is a beautiful city and we enjoyed nights out in the pubs, but I had no idea what people were saying.

I remember asking my new Scottish friends what they wanted to drink. One said, 'Geeza pint o' heavy'. Another preferred what sounded like 'a nippie sweetie' and the third asked for 'a half and half'. I hadn't a clue what those strange-sounding drinks were, so I gave the cash to my Glaswegian pal. He talked to the barman in a language I couldn't understand, then brought the drinks over.

Back in Denmark, I stayed with a friend in Copenhagen. I took a mundane job in a supermarket, but was happy to live in Copenhagen as it's such a fantastic city.

My father was nagging me because, with all my travelling, I seemed to have forgotten about my education. I applied to a teaching college, was accepted and was due to start in August 1986, but the lure of the kibbutz was too much and I headed off to Israel again in July. I spent several weeks there, working and making new friends. One of these was Jimmy; not a Scot but an Australian. He fell in love with me, although I wasn't in love with him. I did like him a lot and was fascinated by his Aussie outlook. But we said our farewells and I returned to Denmark to start my degree.

Several weeks later, I was visiting some friends when their phone rang. It was my mother. 'I've just had a phone call from your friend at the kibbutz,' she said. 'He's hitchhiked all the way from Israel and he's here now.'

She said when she picked Jimmy up from the bus station she guessed who he was immediately. He was dirty looking and unkempt after his travels, so she put him straight in the bath when they arrived home. He was good fun, I admit, and he stayed with us for about a month.

I continued with my studies and Jimmy invited me to Australia the following Christmas. I took up the offer and went to visit him. It was summer and we enjoyed barbecues on the beaches. I just loved the culture; it was such a fun place to be.

Now, I said I wasn't in love with Jimmy, but I did start to grow very fond of him. And so when he proposed I accepted. We were engaged in the awe-inspiring Sydney Tower and I remember looking down at the vast, sprawling city with its beautiful harbour. I gazed into Jimmy's eyes like any excited fiancée, thinking I'd made a good choice.

Jimmy was a lovely man. When I left for Denmark to continue my studies, I was still engaged to him but feeling uneasy about our future. It became obvious that our personalities clashed.

My next visit to Australia, six months later, sadly proved to be the final straw in our relationship. We'd had a bit of a spark, but it seemed to fizzle out during that trip 'down under'. I knew that if I'd really loved him I would have stayed. But the truth was, I didn't. I returned home and never saw Jimmy again.

This time I had to stay put and finish my degree. The last thesis I completed was on macrobiotic cooking. I learned later that Madonna enjoyed this balanced Japanese-style diet. I studied more about macrobiotic techniques at a health centre in Sweden and even put together a cookbook as part of my studies.

My next stop was England again, this time to study acupuncture at a college in East Grinstead. T was also studying acupuncture there, and that's how we met.

I'd just turned 26 and I thought I'd found the man of my dreams. I didn't realise what I was letting myself in for. T was dashing, handsome, intelligent, highly educated – just my type of chap. He was ten years older than me, but I didn't give it a second thought. I found him so attractive. He fancied me too. I guess we were both a bit lonely. I'd just moved to England and hardly knew anyone. We were both looking for a stable relationship and it seemed that we'd met our match.

The fact that T came from Saudi Arabia didn't seem to matter either. Awesome mistake. He wasn't interested in religion. We shared a great passion for Chinese medicine and philosophy, so it seemed rather apt that we should meet on an acupuncture course.

One month later, I was pregnant. Another three months and we were married. I didn't feel at the time I was being a complete idiot, honestly I didn't. Everything just felt so right.

T did talk about his first marriage and how he'd learned from his mistakes. He'd married an English girl when he was 21 and they hadn't had any children. His mother never accepted the marriage, as she wanted him to choose a Saudi wife.

We married in Southampton Register Office on 17 December 1990. The participants on the big day were me, T, his sister and her husband and a friend of T's. Every girl wants a big wedding, but T wanted a small, intimate affair that didn't cost too much. He had a lot of money in the bank – I'd seen his statements – but I went along with the mini-wedding because we were setting up home and it seemed sensible not to waste it.

I wore a blue skirt and a white top. Although I was pregnant, it was such an early stage that I could still wear my normal clothes. The reception involved going back to our house with the others and cooking some food. That was it!

It had come as no surprise to me when T's mother announced that she didn't want to attend the wedding, because I wasn't an Arab girl. She didn't understand our type of relationship. She wanted her son to have an arranged marriage. The only weddings she'd been to were those of her eldest daughter – because she married an Arab – and her third son, Adnan, who married in Saudi Arabia. In fact, she hadn't even wanted to meet me.

To be fair to T, he said to her, 'If you want to keep seeing me, you'll have to accept that I have a new wife.'

I did meet his mother, because we drove to her house in Exeter one weekend. She was pleasant enough, but I could feel the atmosphere between us. I didn't fit in with her expectations, and that was that. I felt that, however hard I tried to be a good wife and a good mother, the fact that I wasn't of Arab descent would always go against me.

I discovered that she was a remarkable woman, stubborn and independent, and, although she didn't like me, I couldn't help but admire her. She collected traditional Bedouin clothes and antique jewellery, and even staged an exhibition at Exeter Museum. She'd also written and self-published several books about traditional Arab costume.

It was in these early days that T said he wanted nothing ever to go wrong with our relationship. I believe he genuinely thought that things would work out wonderfully. I later discovered that, with an Arab man, there are no grey areas; no middle ground. Everything is black or white, with no room for negotiation.

5

BECOMING A MUSLIM

I entered the Muslim world with some trepidation, shortly after the birth in 1996 of my son Adam. I'd picked up some Arabic and read about Islam, but I had no idea what to expect, although I knew I was embarking on a completely different life.

T thought it would be a good idea for me to convert, in case he landed a job in Saudi Arabia. He'd been talking to his brother Adnan, who said there might be work at Jeddah University. T thought we could all go out there for a couple of years, and to do that I needed to become a Muslim. I knew that applying for entry as a Christian would present a wide range of difficulties.

The prospect of becoming a Muslim was exciting, especially as I'd always found it intriguing to explore a new culture. Although T thought my conversion would be a good idea, he didn't push me into it, and in any case my independent nature shone through when it came to making a decision as important as this.

I agreed that T should call the mosque in Exeter and make an appointment for us. We went there one morning and a friendly imam, the head of the mosque, met us at the front entrance. During prayers the imam sits at the front of the mosque but, unlike a Western religious leader, faces the same direction as everyone else – towards Mecca. Even though he leads prayers, he is not considered different from anyone else or, in God's eyes, any better. In fact, if he is too ill to lead prayers, any other person can replace him in this role.

I'd remembered to cover my hair, as is customary when entering a mosque. Once inside we were shown to a room where two Arab-looking men, the witnesses for the occasion, were waiting. The imam had a chat with me about why I wanted to convert to Islam. They continued being friendly, and I thought it was wonderful to be treated in a respectful way. How things were to change a few years later!

The imam read out the first verse of the Qur'an in Arabic. It translates as:

In the name of Allah, the Beneficent, the Merciful.
All praise is due to Allah, the Lord of the Worlds.
The Beneficent, the Merciful.
Master of the Day of Judgement.
Thee do we serve and Thee do we beseech for help.
Keep us on the right path.
The path of those upon whom Thou hast bestowed favours.
Not the path of those upon whom Thy wrath is brought down, nor of those who go astray.

As I repeated this in my broken Arabic, I felt a surge of

excitement, because I've always kept an open mind and sought out new experiences.

And that seemed to be it, although I wondered if I'd have to change my name. Men may take the name of one of the prophets; for example, Muhammad or Abraham. Women can use the name of the prophets' wives. Rena is a popular choice. I learned that I could stick with Helle, as I preferred. I was also told that when a baby is born the parents choose a first name. The second name has to be the father's name, whether it's a boy or a girl. After that comes the grandfather's name and then the family name.

A woman under Islam doesn't change her name to that of her husband. Traditionally she retains her maiden name. I was an exception because T wasn't interested in tradition, and neither was I. It made sense, in England, for me to be called Mrs Amin.

I was about to leave the room when the imam asked if I'd like to meet some of the other women at the mosque and take lessons in Arabic. He wondered also if I'd like to learn more about Islam and the Qur'an. Then he issued me with my conversion paper, which would turn out to be my most valuable document in times of need.

I went along to the mosque again the following Sunday with all my children. T was a bit grumpy for no reason I could see, and he stayed at home. When I entered the mosque with the children and was greeted by some of the ladies, I felt slightly uncomfortable and shy.

The first thing I noticed was that the men and women were separated; it was a case of 'upstairs, downstairs', with me and the other women on the first floor. The men remained downstairs. The children ran excitedly upstairs and I saw dozens of youngsters running around. My boys soon joined in the fun. Hey, this is great! I thought.

Normally, women can take their veils off upstairs. But today was a Sunday and it was 'question time' for the imam. Men weren't allowed to join in as the women formed a discussion group to find out whatever they wanted to know about Islam.

After the group session, it was time for prayers. The imam went downstairs again to the men's section; it was time for Salah, and the imam led the prayers. Only men can lead the prayers.

Five times a day Muslims are asked to stop what they're doing; they could be sleeping or working. The most important thing in a Muslim's life is the relationship with Allah. The ritual prayers improve this relationship. If the prayers are sound and proper, one's deeds will be sound and proper.

In my quest for accuracy, I feel I should quote directly from an Islamic article about the significance of prayer:

'The Muslim faces towards the Ka'bah in Makkah, the symbol of the Oneness of Allah and the unity of Muslims. He stands, bows, and prostrates to his Lord while praising Him, reciting some of the words He revealed in the Qur'an, and asking for His forgiveness and mercy. In doing so, the Muslim reminds himself of his position in the universe as a humble servant of Allah and of his total dependence on his Creator, Cherisher and Sustainer.

'When the Prayer is performed properly – with due humility and remembrance of Allah – it has a lasting effect on the person. It fills his heart with the remembrance of Allah, and with fear of and hope in Him. He will not want to move from that lofty position by disobeying Allah.'

The prayers are 'the second Pillar of Islam' after the Testimony of Faith. As I sat in the Exeter mosque, I could see very clearly that religion was the overriding factor in these people's lives; it meant everything to them.

Wudu, or ablution, is the first step of performing prayer. It's an act of spiritual and physical cleaning, and must be performed before prayer. Without Wudu, no prayer can be accepted.

I began by saying, 'Bismillah Hirrah-man Nirraheem' (In the name of Allah, the Most Beneficent, the Most Merciful). Then I washed my hands up to the wrists three times; rinsed my mouth out three times; carefully sniffed water into my nose three times, blowing it out each time using my left hand. I washed my face from the forehead to the chin, and from ear to ear, three times. After that, starting from the right side, I washed my arm up to the elbow three times and then repeated this for the left arm. With my hands wet, I rubbed them over the top of my head, starting at the forehead and wiping backwards. Using wet fingers, I wiped the inside and outside of my ears. I washed my feet up to the ankles, starting with the right foot.

I ended my prayer by saying: 'Ashadu an la illah ha ill'Allahu wahda hula sharika lah, Wa ashadu ana Muhammadan 'ab duhu wa rasul.' This meant that I was testifying that none had the right to be worshipped except Allah alone. I also testified that Muhammad was his slave and messenger.

Now I was a Muslim in Exeter. But it didn't change anything for me. I didn't see T praying, and he ate bacon and drank beer, so I was hardly going to go the whole hog either. I just continued with my daily life, and my routine was enriched on Sundays when I attended the mosque for ladies' day.

Friday is the main holy day in Islam but in Britain, because of the traditional working week, Sunday is the main day for get-togethers. The boys loved their games with the other children at the mosque. There must have been 30 or 40 children of around their age, all running riot.

And, like me, the boys adored the food. All the women brought the most exquisite dishes. I wasn't sure what to bring, because the culture was relatively new to me, and I didn't think that these sophisticated ladies would appreciate the finer points of my burgers and chips. To be on the safe side, I took along fruit and cakes to share with my newfound friends.

A typical Sunday feast would consist of traditional Arab dishes, such as rice and chicken, hummus, spicy curries and exotic vegetables. They would roll out a long paper tablecloth on the floor and lay out all the food; nearly a hundred people, including the children, chatted, ate and simply soaked up the atmosphere of a beautiful, family-orientated Sunday.

The women carried food to the menfolk downstairs. The men ate in silence, so I could see that we were in the right area of the mosque for entertainment value. It was a fun place on Sundays.

Apart from those Sunday visits, I can't say that I had much more to do with Islam. Women at the mosque did ask me where T was, as he was a Saudi and they expected to see him joining in the prayers. I explained that he was always busy with his work.

The only other time I really went into Muslim mode –

apart from the mosque gatherings – was when T and I were invited to dinner with a Saudi family in Exeter. I wore my scarf, making sure I covered my hair to go into the house. Men and women were separated inside the building. It reminded me of what happened at the mosque. The men congregated in an upstairs bedroom and the women stayed in the lounge with the children. As a newcomer to Islamic ways, I found that odd, but naturally I went along with it all. I admit that I was never comfortable with the separation system. I didn't agree with many of the customs, but I respected what they were doing.

I knew that it all began around AD 610, when Muhammad was asked by the voice of God to deliver a new message to the world. I know that the messages he spread didn't include many of the recently adopted customs. He simply asked women to dress modestly and I don't believe he would have approved of so many modern, hard-line beliefs.

Do women really become better people in the eyes of God if we cover our hair and faces? Did God tell Muhammad that we must be kept away from men and even eat in separate areas of a house?

It's all a matter of interpretation. I'm not saying I'm right; I'm just keeping the debate alive. The recent controversy about veils in the UK made me think back to when I was in Saudi working as a teacher. I followed the story about the Muslim woman who refused to take her veil off while teaching at a school in the north of England. I could never allow my four boys to be taught by someone who was completely covered up. It's not in our culture. I want my kids to see a friendly face and see the mouth moving, so that they pick up on all that the other person is trying to convey.

Of course, I respect that teacher's religion, and I believe that all religions must be respected, but children must be able to see who they're talking to. Her class wouldn't be able to see her lips move, so how could she do her job properly? This is especially important when children are being taught in a language that isn't their native tongue. Even in the Saudi school where I taught, although many of the Arab women covered their hair, they weren't allowed to cover their faces while teaching. It was a mixed school, and men did teach there. Even so, the female teachers made their faces visible at work, even if some covered their faces as they left the school. If the situation had been reversed and I'd wanted to wear my Western clothes in Saudi ... well, no chance.

6

LOVE IS BLIND

I should have steered well clear of Islam. All respect to the devout, but I just didn't know what I was letting myself in for. Goodness, it's so easy in hindsight. Looking at it another way, I have four smashing boys and I wouldn't swap them for anything, so how could I change my past?

Muslims have their way of life. In my opinion and from my experience, it's hard for any non-Muslim to really understand what Islam is all about and its effect on everyday life. If it's not ingrained in your upbringing, I believe it's almost impossible to get your head around it all. So, although I did convert to Islam, I was never going to fit in.

Here's an example of what I mean. When T and I were married and living in Exeter, his brother Adnan arrived to visit with his new wife, Alia. She wore a stunning outfit: a multicoloured floral skirt and top that really caught the eye. Remember, at this stage I knew little of Muslim customs but naturally I tried to make conversation during our first meeting. 'Alia, I really like your dress. It's lovely,' I said.

She gave me an odd look, but didn't say anything. The next day, Adnan gave me a bag with the dress in it. He said it was for me. When I asked him why, he just smiled and walked off.

I was confused. I thought I'd done the right thing, complimenting Alia on her dress; nothing wrong with that, surely? How wrong could I be!

When I asked T what was going on, he explained the Islamic concept of 'the evil eye'. It comes as a bit of a shock at first. If someone gives you the evil eye, it means that they can make bad things happen to you. Harm may come to you, your children, your extended family, your house, your possessions. And all because of the wrong type of glance, which may be an envious one or even one intended to praise. Someone may love you but nevertheless give you the evil eye from a feeling of envy. Whatever the motive of the person giving the evil eye, the receiver will make sudden, dramatic actions.

The episode with Alia is a good example of this. She took off the dress and her husband put it in a box and gave it to me. I should have said to Alia, 'Your dress looks good *on you*.' If I'd said that, there would have been no suggestion of envious intent on my part. My mistake was that, by admiring it, I made it seem that I wanted the dress. So after that I was careful to avoid the risk of a Muslim getting hold of the wrong end of the stick and thinking they'd received the dreaded 'evil eye', as this can lead to big trouble.

When T and I lived in England, we appeared to be a typical

Western couple. I didn't have to wear Arab dress in our daily lives or conform to any Islamic customs. At first, T seemed to accept that I was a modern woman and there was no hint that tensions would arise. I enjoyed wearing trendy clothes and I had – and still have – a passion for handbags and shoes. I was lucky to have a good figure, which I worked hard to maintain after having four children. I would let my long, blonde hair flow freely if I had the chance to ride in an open-topped sports car. I liked nothing better than going out for a drink and a meal, and I looked forward to visiting a club or the cinema. I'd done all this as a single woman and I expected to continue to do so with my partner even after we had children. But we started to have a family early in our marriage and after that T didn't want to go out anywhere.

I enjoy going out with people of all types. Some might think I'm flirty and tactile, but that's just me and I'd be happy to see the same qualities in my partner. I'd still remain committed to that one person, and anyone who knows me could vouch for that. I have an exceptionally determined nature. And, despite all the problems that developed, I was committed to working hard at saving our marriage.

In truth, the Muslim way of life had brought a series of shocks from the very start. By the time of my conversion, of course, I understood about the need to cover my head when entering a mosque. But, when I first learned of this custom, it came as a complete surprise. A week after our wedding, we had to attend a mosque in London to have it registered. We drove there in T's red VW Golf and parked outside.

As we were about to get out of the car, he said, 'Where's your scarf?'

'What scarf?' I asked.

'Don't you know that you have to cover your hair to walk into the mosque?' he said.

I was stunned, and turned around with my face wearing what must have looked like a great big question mark. T looked irritated and started fumbling about in the back of the car, trying to find something to cover my hair. He discovered a sarong-sized cloth, a scarf-like thing which I thought he used for checking his oil. He told me to put it over my hair. I didn't have a clue how to arrange it on my head in Muslim style, but I thought I'd done a reasonable job.

However, the situation quickly deteriorated. It was a very windy December day and, as I walked up to the mosque, the makeshift scarf fell off. I struggled to put it back on and I suppose I must have looked absolutely ridiculous.

I trotted after my husband into the mosque. We were told that we needed witnesses for the occasion, and two men appeared out of nowhere to do the honours.

After the ceremony, T said he'd been told by the people there that he shouldn't have married me. Now, there's a confidence-booster if I ever heard one.

My family also wanted to arrange a celebration for me in Denmark, so we flew there at Christmas and T met my friends and relatives. He put on a charming performance and everyone liked him. We were staying at my sister's house and while there I felt ill and was sick for the first time during my pregnancy. T wanted sex, but I told him I felt terrible. He replied, 'When your husband wants sex, it is your duty to provide it.'

It was by no means the last time I would be told to do my

duty. Do my duty? All this 'duty' business was already starting to get to me. I should have listened to a little voice in the back of my head that said, 'Helle, something is going to go horribly wrong here.' In time, that lone voice became a chorus, although I did obey to a certain extent. I had to, if the marriage was to stand any chance of surviving.

Early on, our relationship was put under further heavy strain by what I consider a stupid move on T's part. There he was, studying acupuncture in East Grinstead, working away happily towards his qualification. Then he broke the rules. He set up a Saturday-morning clinic in Southampton – unlicensed – and didn't keep it a secret. The college found out and held a big meeting about T's misdemeanour. He was called in and told he was being expelled. As I was studying at the same place, I felt that I too had no option but to leave. T transferred to another college in London, but because it operated a different system he had to repeat an entire year, with all the costs that entailed.

I should explain that T told me early on that he could never live in Saudi Arabia, although that was the country of his birth. He left there to live in Egypt when he was very young, and then the family moved to England when he was only eight years old. So he never really grew up with Saudi customs, although his mother spoke to him only in Arabic.

The idea was for T and his brothers and sisters to be educated in England and eventually return to Saudi. Arab culture stresses the importance of education and T's mother realised that to put them through a school in England would be the ideal choice. But how could his mother support seven children here without any financial help? Well, T's father owned a successful travel agency and organised pilgrimages to Mecca from many countries. He earned more than enough to provide for his family.

T and his siblings certainly had a variety of backgrounds. When T and his younger brother obtained their doctorates, they left for Saudi Arabia and were employed as professorial assistants at Jeddah University. However, after four years T had had enough of the country. He was getting itchy feet and returned to England to study acupuncture. His brother stayed in Saudi and married. His eldest sister went to America and did likewise. The eldest brother qualified as a doctor, married an Irish woman and returned to Saudi. They had four children who all went to boarding school in England. His other two sisters married Englishmen and stayed here. The youngest sister lived with her mother most of her life and, I believe, never married.

T always told me he didn't have a good time in Saudi Arabia and would never want to live there again. I believe he meant it at the time, but when push came to shove he thought he'd be safe with the kids there. In other circumstances, that might have been true, but it would turn out to be a different matter with me on his case.

When I first met T, I had only a vague idea of where Saudi Arabia was. I knew it was hot there, with lots of desert, oil and money. But hey, who cared ... I had found my man. And I remember my friends saying, 'Wow, Helle, he's a real catch. He's good-looking, intelligent and he'll have plenty of money.' Well, most of that was true.

Early in our relationship, I discovered that T was interested in all forms of religion. He was obviously a Muslim, but he didn't pray or go to the mosque. We enjoyed bacon, ham, beer, wine and everything that Islam deplored.

LOVE IS BLIND

The fact that he was a Muslim and I was a Christian didn't seem to matter at all. At that stage, there seemed to be no conflict of interests on any level.

T could really turn on the charm. I was under his spell, it seemed, and in my eyes he could do nothing wrong. I can't say I was totally in love with him, but I was certainly besotted and fascinated.

In retrospect, I should have waited and known him a lot better before committing myself and having children. However, I have an impulsive nature and, with T, it got the better of me. And then along came the kids.

7

TROUBLE IN PARADISE

The twins Mahmoud and Faisal, who later changed their names to Max and Alex, were born on 17 June 1991. It was a lovely pregnancy, even though my belly grew big very quickly and I didn't know I was expecting twins until rather late in the day. At this point in my life, I wasn't into conventional pre-natal care, so I hadn't had a scan or other pre-natal tests.

T and I had been planning a home birth, but things didn't turn out that way. Thirty-two weeks into the pregnancy, I developed severe back pain. A scan revealed that I was having twins. At 34 weeks, my waters broke early in the morning and I went into labour. T rushed me to the maternity unit at the Princess Anne Hospital in Southampton.

I remember doctors and nurses rushing around, because they knew they were dealing with premature twins. They didn't know what state the babies would be in. Max came out slightly anaemic. Alex appeared ten minutes later, bright red and screaming. I was shown the children for about two seconds before they were rushed off to the premature baby unit. It was a dramatic entrance into the world for them, but the hospital staff were fantastic. I was thrilled to have had a natural birth. And no stitches!

Max and Alex were healthy identical twins, although both very small at about three and a half pounds. I was determined to breastfeed them, but I was advised by doctors at the hospital to go home and leave the boys in their care.

The twins were due to go on formula milk. The doctors said I could come and visit them daily and take them home when they'd gained enough weight. *No way* was I having that – I refused to leave my babies. Typical of me, I made a huge fuss and managed to stay put for a fortnight. My stubborn streak shone through again.

T and I had a discussion about the boys' names. I wanted to give them English names, because I thought it would be easier for them living in England. T was having none of it. He was the father and he decided on the names. Full stop.

According to tradition, T's first son had to be called after his own father, Mahmoud. The name means 'the gifted one'. I predicted he would indeed be gifted, but I didn't like the name one single bit. I thought of many attractive alternatives, but T wouldn't budge.

I had no idea about Arab names, but I liked the sound of 'Faisal' and its meaning: he would have the strength of a sword. Years later, after they were abducted, the boys wanted to change their names to fit in with their Western pals. T still calls them Mahmoud and Faisal and won't accept their decision to change their names.

I persisted with my attempts to breastfeed the twins and before long it was going well. I managed to feed them for five months with no other kinds of milk or supplements. Then they went on to sheep's and goat's milk, which I collected from local farms. I proudly donated nearly four pints of breast milk to the hospital, to use for other premature babies. When we returned home, after two weeks, I was feeling rather worn out.

Reality hit me as soon as I walked through the front door. The house was a mess. T had decided to bring down a lot of stuff from the loft and had left it for me to sort out. He also needed me to take over the kitchen again. Now that I was home, he expected me to cook every meal for him. What was more, they had to be perfect every time. But by now I was in full swing, breastfeeding and caring for my babies, cooking, cleaning and tidying for hours, and taking care of all T's needs. And at times these seemed to be greater than those of my babies put together.

T appeared to have in his head exactly how he wanted everything to be. His first marriage had failed and now he was implementing a plan of action for us. He didn't seem to be in touch with the needs of the people around him – especially me. I could see that he was afraid of losing control.

Whenever we had people over, T would run around and do everything. As soon as we were alone, I was in charge of it all again. My studies went out of the window, whereas T was travelling up to London to complete his repeated year at college.

I used to accuse him of being far too mean. I'll never forget one incident in particular. We were given a second-hand twin pushchair that broke after about four months. Without it, I was stuck in the house. I was used to being independent, so it made me depressed.

Six weeks went by, and still no replacement pushchair appeared. When we went out together, we had to carry the babies in slings. T wouldn't fork out for a new pushchair and kept looking in the newspaper for a cheaper model. While he managed to get out and about in his car, a pushchair was no great issue for him.

One weekend, T travelled up to London and I felt so upset not being able to leave the house. Then I remembered I had some money in an account in Denmark. I called my mum and asked her to send it to me. Right, I thought, I have to take charge here. I called my friend Caroline and asked her if I could borrow money until the cash came from Denmark. It was that independent streak again.

We arranged for Caroline's mum to come over and mind the boys, while Caroline took me shopping at the John Lewis store in Southampton. I was soon the proud owner of a Silver Cross, at that time the Mercedes of pushchairs. It was the all-singing, all-dancing model, and the best value for £300 I can remember.

The first thing T saw on his return from London was the new pushchair parked in the kitchen. He was furious.

'How dare you do something like that without asking me first,' he barked.

'You should have listened to me,' I told him. 'I wasn't prepared to sit looking at these four walls for another day. I've been waiting for another pushchair for six weeks.'

T stomped off and didn't speak to me for two days.

Max and Alex were active, happy little boys, always up to mischief. With big smiles on their little faces all the time, they were very sociable and interacted well with other kids.

When the twins were a year old, we moved from Southampton to Exeter. T wanted to be near his mother and, to start with, we lived with her. I hated every minute there.

Issa, who later changed his name to Zak, was conceived at T's mother's house. We bought a new home in the middle of Exeter and Zak was born there. I had a wonderful pregnancy with him. I went into labour three weeks early. T was great during labour and delivery, as he had been with Max and Alex.

During Zak's birth, the twins were looked after at a neighbour's house. Only a midwife, a student midwife and T were present. The doctor couldn't make it in time. Well, we didn't need one. Zak was the most perfect, content and beautiful child. It was a piece of cake having just one baby instead of two at once.

Just before Zak was born, T discovered shamanism, which is a mix of ancient beliefs and practices. He went on a spiritual journey to the 'underworld' and met Zak as an old man in a cave. T asked the old man what he wanted to be called in this lifetime. 'Issa,' was his answer. So my new son would be called Issa, though only for a few years, of course. It's the Arabic name for Jesus. Muslims believe that Jesus was one of many prophets.

Zak adored his mummy. He was breastfed for almost two years; very different from the twins. He was happiest at home just toddling around next to me.

When Zak was almost three, and Max and Alex coming

up for five, Adnan – named after T's brother, although later he would change his name to Adam – was born. He wasn't exactly planned, but I was delighted to be pregnant.

Adam was also born at home. He was a full-term baby and therefore bigger than the others were. I was a good eight hours in labour before he finally appeared, and it was a much harder birth than my other deliveries. The midwife told me that, statistically, the third pregnancy was the hardest and the most likely to have complications. Despite all that, I had no real problems with Adam's birth.

He was a lovely baby. Although he had brown eyes, his skin was much lighter than the other boys'. Sitting with my new baby in my arms and having his brothers around me, it suddenly felt like I had a lot of children. I was tired. It was hard work and T was very demanding. He was at home much of the time but only helped with the boys, housework and cooking when he chose to. I could never rely on him.

Around the time of Adam's birth, an au pair girl from Denmark came to stay with us. We found her through my sister back home, who knew a girl who wanted to travel abroad for this sort of work. One day I went to collect something from her room and saw her diary was open. I shouldn't have looked, but I did.

Her latest entry said she was very unhappy; she described T as a domineering, bad-tempered man. 'I don't know how she puts up with him,' it said. I remember she wrote that if things didn't improve she'd look for another family. I felt shocked and upset that someone viewed my husband in this light. I felt I had accepted and was used to everything about my marriage to T, but this diary pulled no punches.

Looking back, I can honestly say that I did my best to

meet everyone's needs and demands. I felt I had created a happy environment for my boys to grow up in. My biggest regret is that I let T dominate and control me. I compromised all the time and I gave in most of the time.

When I left T mother's house for our new home in Exeter, I felt liberated, if that was possible in my circumstances. I adored our picturesque detached house, which sat proudly in the centre of the city. It had a garden, a drive and an imposing wrought-iron gate at the front.

At the same time, three years into our marriage, I had become desperate for everything to work out. I hated our bickering, which seemed all the worse because I was so busy with the children. Most couples endure some of this, I knew, so I was trying to ignore it and enjoy what we had.

That year, T and I set up a health centre for alternative therapies in our new home.

One room was used for the practice and the rest of the house was for family use. Even though T and I weren't getting on very well, I was quite enthusiastic about the venture because I could see some professional possibilities. It was all his idea. He practised acupuncture and I specialised in aromatherapy. Initially, my only misgiving was that it would have been better to work away from the house. After a while, I grew disenchanted with the arrangement because, working and living together under the same roof, there was so little personal space, and this brought further strain.

That wasn't all. T went on a weekend course in shamanism and then advertised himself as giving lessons in the subject. And, although a lot of potential students responded to the ad, he also received angry phone calls from people who had studied and practised shamanism for many years and were upset about his setting up as a teacher after a two-day course.

The business made a slow start, and, although it picked up and indeed carried on for five years, takings were never high. What troubled me more than our business, though, was that T never seemed to be settled. His background was completely different from mine and it showed in our attitudes towards many issues. He would see my place as being in the kitchen, doing everything around the house and with the children. Then there was his constant need to be in control of everything, me included.

We agreed we needed a change. We thought a holiday in Bali might help, and the brochures certainly looked encouraging. Six weeks, maybe, to patch things up. By now, we had four children and our relationship was feeling worn out.

T was bored by Exeter and I could tell he needed to move on. His sister, who ran a successful frozen-food factory in Chester, encouraged him to move up there and join the company. We formed a plan to sell the house in Exeter, put our belongings in storage and take a holiday in Bali. After that, we'd move up to Chester. Well, it seemed a good idea at the time, but things didn't work out exactly as planned ...

Our holiday in Bali seemed to get us back on track. So, just a month after returning to rainy England and living under a cloud at T's mother's house, we were back on the tropical island once more. T had spotted an opportunity to run a furniture business, but, like our marriage, it was doomed from the start.

He'd taken too much on; he struggled to cope when we converted the business into a school; we started to argue more and more, and the worse things became, the less he would listen. He didn't want to know what I had to say.

I knew for sure that our marriage was heading for the rocks a few weeks before I turned 36. We were working on designs for the interior layout of the villa, our brand new home in Bali. I could see that rooms were going in the wrong places, and the house was going to be a crazy place to live in.

I had a look at the plans for our bedroom and saw that the toilet was on the opposite side of the room to the shower. I thought I could nip this one in the bud with a quick drawing, and a few well-meant suggestions. Interior design has always been one of my hobbies, so I went to work and designed an en suite instead of bits and pieces all over the room.

When I showed T my alternative layout, I was bubbling with enthusiasm and brimming over with ideas. After all, I thought, this was my home as well and I had to live in it.

'Hey, T, have a look at this, you might find it interesting,' I suggested, trying to open the negotiations with a flourish.

He reluctantly glanced at my work and did show a flicker of interest. Deciding I would capitalise on the fact that I had his attention, I rapidly suggested other ideas for the kitchen, the walls, the garden. I tried to fit as much information in as I could, relishing my new role as design adviser.

After his two-minute silence to consider my ideas, I was put firmly back in my place. 'So you fancy yourself as some sort of interior designer, do you? Helle, you know nothing about building, you know nothing about interior design and you know nothing about anything, really. I think you should stick to domestic duties and look after the children.

83

How about going to the kitchen and making me some tea? If we're going to avoid disaster, you'd better leave the important decisions to me.'

I should have been devastated by that and I should have been crying floods of tears. I should have felt a great sense of injustice. But I was so used to being treated like a dog that I just brushed it off. I screwed up my little drawing and threw it in the bin.

T hardly spoke to me for the rest of the day. When he did acknowledge my presence, barbed comments flew in my direction but I didn't bother arguing. We didn't exchange a word, not even a glance, when we went to bed.

Surprise, surprise, the next morning, T was in a bubbly mood. He looked as if he'd had a few ideas about the villa. He was full of suggestions and, as he went through them, I noticed that they all sounded rather familiar. They were my ideas and he was claiming the lot! I just went along with it all and praised him for his wonderful ideas. I was only looking at the end result: a house fit to live in.

I knew that the layout of the bedroom wouldn't make any impact on our strained relationship; I didn't want to get laid there anyway. He slept facing one way and I was happy to face the opposite direction. Sex was never on the agenda. We argued so much that there was no touching, no intimacy, and I didn't really want sex with him in any case.

Our marriage began to fade out completely around the middle of 2000. Our bedroom encounters were a rare event, but I noticed that the number of condoms in his drawer was reducing rapidly. That was our chosen method of contraception at the time but, with sex off the agenda, the chances of becoming a mum again were nil.

I remembered seeing a full packet of condoms; then I saw half a packet; and then there were just two condoms left. Maybe I was hallucinating. Maybe I'd miscounted. Maybe I was right and they were disappearing. But where were they going? I decided to keep quiet, as my evidence was flimsy.

I also kept quiet about another incident. One day I came home and saw him pack his gym bag. Then he went out to the car with it and came back indoors. Something seemed odd about this.

I had a spare key to his car, so I furtively sneaked out and had a look. I opened the bag and saw all the usual sports clothes. But when I put my hand deep inside I came across a pile of condoms. I was sure he wasn't going to a balloon party; maybe he was planning some sort of marathon sex session.

You can imagine how I felt. I didn't have anyone I could talk to. Most of my friends on the island had connections with both the school and T, so I had to bottle it all up inside.

During the next month, T became more abusive. He went out every night and came back late. We hardly communicated. It was just horrible.

He didn't seem to care about me at all. I drove an Espace and he had a 4x4. My car broke down and sat outside the house for five weeks. I kept nagging T to get it fixed. Then I realised that he felt he was more in control if I didn't have a car. He did all the driving, took the children everywhere and knew everything that was going on. I remained stuck in the house.

When a local odd-job man dropped some equipment off for the swimming pool, I asked him if he'd have a look at the car. After taking a peek inside the bonnet, he concluded that there wasn't much wrong. He suggested I use the local garage, a few hundred yards up the road. I gave him a tip and he headed off to tell the garage about my plight.

Within an hour, an obliging mechanic arrived. He checked over the Espace and spotted the problem within a minute. The spark plugs were dirty. He cleaned them and ten minutes later he was on his way with 20,000 rupees in his back pocket. I'd paid him a couple of pounds sterling; not much to secure my freedom once more.

I was so proud of myself for getting the job done. It was the day before my birthday and I reckoned it would be my only present. As I admired the car, running sweetly outside the house, T arrived back from school.

'Who moved the car?' he asked sharply. I could sense the anger building in his voice.

'I had it fixed for £2,' I said, trying to justify my actions in a matter-of-fact voice. 'I'm fed up of being stuck in the house all day, not able to go anywhere or do anything.'

'How dare you do things to the car without my permission!' he hit back.

I could feel rage growing inside, but I didn't want a confrontation as the kids had just arrived home from school.

T stomped off to his car and reappeared carrying an ugly large sheet of brown plastic. I watched him bring it into the house and fit it over the swimming pool. I took several deep breaths to try to control my fury, and walked over to find out what on earth he was up to.

'The pool has to be covered when it's not in use. I can save money on the chemicals.'

I had no idea what he was on about; nor did the teachers at the school when he covered the pool there as well. Apart from being puzzled about the chemicals issue, we all thought the cover was dangerous as children might get trapped underneath it. It was just another of T's crazy ideas, I suppose.

T completed his mission at the pool and sat down on the sofa in the lounge. I couldn't contain myself any longer. Seeing me striding over, he looked upwards in a 'tut-tut' style, as if he was going to have to put up with more nonsense from me.

'We need to talk now,' I rasped, standing in front of him with my arms crossed.

'I've nothing to talk to you about,' he replied with a glare.

'Well, I have something to talk to you about,' I snarled. Yes, I do believe I snarled as I began to boil over, and there must have been a contorted expression on my face, finely honed by many years of a miserable marriage.

I screamed and screamed at him, paced up and down the room and then screamed some more. He continued to look skywards; his eyes just rolled and no other muscle in his body moved an inch.

'Firstly, I refuse to live for one more minute with that plastic sheet on my swimming pool,' my tirade began. 'Everything you have brought into our marriage is ugly and negative. I want that thing off my swimming pool now. I hate every day of my life with you. You make the children's and my life a misery.

'I'd like you to explain to me right now why there are two condoms left in the drawer next to our bed. Where are the others? I haven't used them. The only person who uses condoms around here is you. I, as your wife, demand an explanation.

'I looked in your gym bag and found a whole load of condoms in there. Do you use them at the gym? Is there a new exercise, involving condoms, that I don't know about?'

I continued like a dog with a very juicy bone and could feel myself gathering strength as I laid into him. 'Are you having an affair? Are you sleeping with another woman? If you are, I will never ever sleep with you again. I am no longer your doormat. I refuse to live like this for one more day. How dare you treat me like this.'

It read like a savage prepared statement, but all the incidents of the past few years came together and I just gave vent to my feelings. I listed and commented venomously on every grievance as I continued screaming at my husband.

I returned to the issue of the missing condoms and whether this meant he was having an affair.

'What do you expect, with a wife like you?' he said eventually, in a rattled-sounding voice. He was trying to stay cool and collected, but that's not how he came across.

'You're skinny, dried up, miserable and so unattractive. I don't fancy you any more and I don't love you any more either,' he added.

The words cut through me like a knife. It wasn't as if I had any love left for him, but his choice of words still pierced my heart.

'Right then, I will never sleep with you in the same bed ever again and I will never have sex with you again, you bastard.'

I didn't regret what I'd said. My birthday was the next day, but I wasn't expecting a romantic weekend for two on an idyllic Indonesian island. That wasn't going to happen anyway. On the plus side, my rant had certainly made my position clear.

I went to the bedroom, collected all my possessions and moved into a room on the top floor. I felt stronger because of what I'd done, but at the same time I was shaky and wondered what the repercussions might be.

I had a peek out of my new room, as I could see T was on the move outside. I watched him take the hideous brown sheet off the swimming pool, fold it up and throw it in the corner of the garden. Then he stormed up to my room and screamed at me – doubtless in retribution for my previous outburst.

'Right, Helle, have it your way. You can clean the swimming pool. From now on, I won't touch it. You buy the chemicals, you clean the thing out. I'm not lifting a finger.'

'That's no problem,' I told him. 'Just show me what to do. I'll enjoy cleaning out the pool.'

'I'm showing you nothing,' he shot back at me. 'You want to do it, you work out how to do it. Give me your car keys. I'll do the driving around here.'

I remember what I was thinking at this stage. Does a woman really deserve all this? Do I deserve all this? Why is my life such a nightmare? How can I escape? Is this the man I married? I sensed that if we split up it was all going to end up in some sort of court battle, but I also knew that right was on my side. I wanted to be left alone. I gave him the keys.

Unfortunately, the kids heard both of our screaming sessions. I felt really bad about that and wished we'd been able to row in private. But, even though there were four children around, situations developed and I had no control over how they started and ended.

I woke up on my birthday, 22 August 2001. Outside, the

sun kept up its perpetual hot glow. Inside my heart, it was as cold as ice. The only comfort I felt was cuddling up to little Adam, who shared my bed with me.

It was a school day, so I prepared for my usual routine. A quick scan around the house revealed no sign that there was a birthday anywhere. There was nothing from T, not that I wanted anything. The kids were too small to be thinking about handing out cards. I hated my birthday already, and morning had only just broken.

I went downstairs to get the breakfast table ready with the maid. T appeared with a face as black as the blackest thundercloud one could imagine. He didn't say a word and he didn't look at me as he sat down at the table and ordered what he wanted from the maid.

When I told the kids it was my birthday, they were more than excited. They sang 'Happy Birthday' for me, and asked what I wanted to do on my big day.

'You must have a birthday party, Mummy,' Max insisted, as he gave me his tenth hug of the morning.

An idea began to hatch. I did really want a birthday party, if I could possibly have one. In Denmark, birthdays are important occasions marked by extravagant parties. So how was I going to do it and who was I going to invite?

One attribute of mine is the ability to make something out of the worst situation imaginable: to turn a negative into a positive. The party looked a no-hoper, but hey!

I compiled a guest list and made a few phone calls. Some mums wanted to come and I also invited some of the teachers. Soon the list had expanded to ten, not including the kids. I wasn't interested in what T thought. I was on a roll, it was my birthday and I was looking forward to my party. I arranged the knees-up for four o'clock, leaving about seven hours to get things organised.

I carried out my weekly count-up and realised that I had very little money. I had about £5 worth of local currency. I didn't have my car, so a trip to the supermarket was out of the question. I raided the fridge, freezer and cupboards and assembled all the useful ingredients I could find. Then I compiled a list that seemed designed to test the local shop to the limit. They came up with eggs, flour, butter, icing sugar and balloons. Sorted.

My feast was taking shape. By the time the boys arrived home from school, I had made cakes, biscuits and sandwiches. I transformed the dining room into a party zone; balloons floated around everywhere and it became one happy spot in the house for a day.

The boys made cards at school and delivered them to their proud mum. My guests started to arrive, bearing cards and presents. I was astonished to see T walk in with an enormous bunch of flowers. My mum had sent them to the school. T threw them down on the table and stomped off.

They say love is blind. Now, though, I could see.

8

LIFE IN BALI

My first experience of Bali was my holiday there with T and the boys, and it was a good one. Later, with my family living on the island, all the drama unfolded.

When we set up the furniture business in Bali, I thought T's company might not fare too well. I just couldn't see him as an entrepreneur. I came from a business-minded family and I knew that T's talents lay elsewhere. For example, he was a skilful acupuncturist and excelled at giving lectures on the subject.

I can see why T was attracted to the island. Bali is like a focal point for Indonesian businesses. Companies from other parts of the region send their goods there for sale. Thousands of buyers arrive to snap up the best-quality teak tables, beds, garden furniture and genuine antiques, mainly from Java.

Yet I just couldn't imagine T dealing with customers, keeping books, managing staff and all the rest of it. If he'd listened to me, taken on board some of my ideas and let me have some input, things may have turned out differently. I wanted us to work together, but instead he shut me out of everything to do with the business. That was his way; my job was to organise life at home.

'Why don't you start small?' I suggested as I gazed with incredulity at a massive showroom taking shape. 'Then you can test the market and maybe go on from there. Hundreds of people are in the same line of business as you. What about some market research first?'

He looked at me as if I was an idiot. Already I knew that the monstrous building was going to be a white elephant. I could even visualise a pair of tusks sticking out of the top.

We hardly sold any furniture. It was all too expensive and his goods weren't right for the market. I take no pleasure in saying I was right.

Despite everything that happened to me there, I have some wonderful memories of Bali. It is a beautiful place and its people are friendly, happy and innocent. In some ways, I fell in love with the island. Sometimes, though, I hated being there. It's great taking a holiday in Bali, but trying to integrate into the community is a stressful job. I felt under pressure all the time, and T was always stressed out trying to get to grips with Bali business tactics. All of a sudden, England seemed a million miles away.

Educating the kids was my priority, of course. At this time, their ages ranged from three to eight, and I was lucky to discover a small study group run by an Australian teacher, Marie. It was held in a small house with a tiny classroom and a little yard. My boys received one-to-one tuition, a bit of a rarity in their future schools.

Marie used books brought in from England, and I helped out, along with some of the other mums. It was a lovely way of providing education for my children, and such a tranquil setting. I never imagined that ahead of us there would be seven schools before we returned to England.

As soon as I arrived in Bali, I was fascinated; so much so that I helped to compile a travel guide to the place, as part of the Eyewitness series published by Dorling Kindersley. The job came to me via one of the mums at the school, Sarah Dougherty.

She's an Australian journalist who worked and lived in Bali while I was there. Sarah was commissioned by Dorling Kindersley to compile a hotel and restaurant guide to the islands of Bali and Lombok. She was pregnant at the time and needed urgent research carried out. So, while the kids were at school in the mornings, I zoomed around the island checking out the resorts, hotels and restaurants.

I was excited when Sarah asked me to become involved, but I had to be careful not to disclose everything to T. He hated my role in the project, because it meant I was away from the house and not doing the cooking. Normally, maids would cook and do all the household chores, but T insisted that I should wear the apron, because it kept me in the home and, from his point of view, out of mischief. It was that control thing again.

When talking to him about the travel guide, I tried to play down my commitment, but it was a substantial project. Before it was finished, Sarah left to have her baby in Australia. That meant a really hectic schedule for me, and even then I couldn't visit everywhere. Local professional people, secretaries for example, were hired to do some of the work in the more remote areas.

We reviewed accommodation ranging from the most flamboyant, five-star hotels to the cheapest hostels. Most were falling over themselves to get in the guide, so we were inundated with free lunches, spa sessions and a whole lot more. We also compiled the restaurant section in the book, so I enjoyed fabulous free meals for three months.

As well as hotels to suit all budgets, Bali has countless stunning beaches. The one that stands out is Sanur Beach, only ten minutes' drive from Denpasar. The eager sun-worshipper gets there early, finds a clean spot, lazes on the dazzling white sand and watches the sun rise. Sanur was one of the first resorts developed on the island, so the area has maintained its traditions. Not far from the beach, ancient temples live and breathe centuries of worship and tradition.

Those who want to escape the hustle and bustle of the popular beach resorts can escape to the northern tip of the island. You come across a stretch of villages by the Bali Sea and a wonderful stretch of coastline called Lovina Beach. Not far from the beach you will find hot springs, waterfalls and clear water for snorkelling and diving.

There's a down side, as you'd expect. Each resort and beach seems more alluring than the last, and in the main tourist areas they do their best to keep tidying up the rubbish. But, elsewhere, things aren't so pristine.

Because it's still a Third World country, rubbish of all types gets dumped in the sea. Most people don't know what to do with it. I used to show my maids the difference between throwing away a banana skin and a plastic bottle. I explained that the banana came from nature and would rot back into the environment, whereas a bottle or tin can would lie on the beach for many years. I tried to make them understand, but didn't have much success.

So, if you go swimming away from the main resorts, prepare for a tide of scum and bottles to greet you in the water. Thousands of them bob up and down on the waves. I used to pick up hundreds, but soon realised that many more were waiting to take their place.

It's only fair to warn the unwary that sometimes what floats by is even worse. Bali is a beautiful place but, like many islands of its type, it does cast an unfortunate shadow on the environment.

I remember going to a secluded beach not far from a ferry terminal. All the children were playing happily, and I was watching the ferries coming and going. I saw a large brown slick, maybe 60 feet across, floating ominously towards the beach. We could tell what it was without further investigation.

Pollution and overfishing are destroying coral reefs throughout the world, and Bali is no exception. The more damage caused, the more the environment suffers. Efforts are being made to reverse this carnage, for the long-term health of our planet.

I blame dynamite fishing for much of the damage. I've seen it happening, and can believe a United Nations-backed report that says 86 per cent of Indonesia's coral reefs are under threat. The blasting techniques are banned, of course, but we're dealing with Third World attitudes here. How do we get the message over to the people?

I find it horrifying that an illegal fisherman can fill up an empty bottle with fertiliser and kerosene, light it and throw it into the ocean. Hundreds of dead fish appear, and he has a huge catch for the day. Reefs are often destroyed from the inside, leaving no room for regrowth. I heard the *boom-boom* of the fishermen's underhand tactics, and I knew that another vital part of the environment had been blasted into oblivion.

Where there is life, although fragile, there has to be hope. A chain of islands lies to the east of Bali. They're known as the Nusa Tengarra and include Sumbawa, Sumba, Flores, Timor and Lombok. Bali is lush compared with Lombok. It's drier there, the landscape is rugged and the coastline has been fighting a losing battle against mankind.

I don't know if they'll still be there when you read this, but pink marker buoys off Lombok are the evidence of an innovative programme to save threatened coral reefs. New habitats have been created, not only there but also in other vulnerable parts of Indonesia. You can compare a reef to a rainforest when it comes to diversity of life. A reef is home to many species of fish and other organisms. Scientists took samples from one sheltered Indonesian island and found 1,100 species of fish and 450 types of coral. We damage that wildlife system at our peril.

Here's how the project works. So-called 'coral arks' create new havens for fish and corals where humans have eroded the natural environment. An artificial reef has been built, using steel bars and copper wiring. A low-voltage current is transmitted into the seawater. Minerals in the water crystallise and form a limestone coating over the steel. This in turn attracts coral larvae. To give the process a natural helping hand, fragments from healthier reefs are attached to the structure. I see that similar schemes are under way in other parts of the world, and their success or failure may ultimately affect us all.

When I was on holiday in Bali, and later while living

there, I realised that some of the landscape has to be seen to be believed. For example, volcanoes attract thousands of tourists every year. These awesome landmarks run through the centre of the island and are believed by the local population to be the home of the gods.

The island's main volcano, Gunung Agung, is still active. It's considered sacred by the Balinese, who see it as the centre of the universe. The peak is nearly 10,000 feet high and means as much to the Balinese as Olympus would have done to the Ancient Greeks. I was told that islanders always sleep with their heads towards Agung. I never tried that, but my sense of direction is appalling, so that ritual wouldn't have worked for me.

There are smaller, and more user-friendly Gunungs. I climbed Gunung Batur, a peak that still erupts regularly (not when I was in the vicinity, fortunately). It's a half-day trek up a steep hill, but the views in the early morning take some believing. I remember gazing across at the other peaks and looking down at lakes through a carpet of mist.

There are many less strenuous walks on the island where you can take in waterfalls, rows of rice paddies and dense tropical forests (my God, I hope they're still there). I do disagree with some of the tourist brochures, though. I read that walkers encounter a chorus of birds in the wilderness. I was even told to look out for the rare Bali starling. I never came across many birds and I believe it's because so many are caught and sold to pet shops.

Balinese love-song birds command high prices. I encountered a lively trade in dogs, tropical fish, crickets and fighting cocks. It's a sad fact that if you have money you can buy any creature, even if the species is endangered.

I must add that when I visited a market I saw birds of all shapes and sizes kept in cages in terrible conditions. I felt sick when I looked at them, all colourful and proud in their tiny cages, but I could see that many were dying. I visited the market only once.

On the bright side, I saw animal charities buying the birds to set them free. I rejoiced when I saw this happen, but then felt downhearted when the birds were caught once more and taken to market.

I was also more than a little concerned to learn about the area's volatile geology, with fault lines that threaten to cause earthquakes and volcanic eruptions. Tourist books tell you that Indonesia is a ring of fire and a circle of trouble surrounding the Pacific. Mind you, I had enough eruptions going off in my own life to counter anything offered up by the volcanoes.

The island has suffered from deforestation, with farmers clearing their land of trees. Indigenous specimens have been preserved in the nature reserves, and mangrove forests have been replanted, and so that form of conservation is high on the action list there.

The Balinese speak more English than the people of most other parts of Indonesia. I imagine that's because they've been exposed to more international tourism. Despite so many foreign influences, they've managed to preserve their culture. The average tourist has the option of surfing, sailing, scuba diving and white-water rafting.

The people of Bali are in a class of their own. They always greet you with a smile on their faces. No matter how poor, how unfortunate or afflicted, they'll always give you their best.

And the children always have to be on their best behaviour. To the outsider it may seem as if they're super-well behaved, compared with Western kids. But the way they're brought up explains this. They learn that if they misbehave the bogeyman will get them. They must behave, otherwise the gods and spirits won't be pleased. A unique religion based on Hinduism is practised in Bali, although the island also has many Muslims and Christians.

You could say that our first house – before we built the villa – was at the crossroads of all religions. We rented the place, in the middle of a small village. It had no hot water, not even a proper kitchen and it was pretty basic.

Thirty feet from my living-room window was a Pentecostal church, with its singing, dancing and audience involvement. I was so close to the congregation I could have joined in.

We also had a mosque in the village, calling the faithful to prayer five times a day. I'm sure that their loudspeakers were pointing directly at my bedroom. Also in the village, we had a Hindu temple, with others scattered throughout the area. They made a significant contribution to the ambient volume.

Ceremonies abound on the island. For example, when a Balinese baby is born, the umbilical cord is placed in the village shrine. When the person dies, the preserved cord is reunited with its owner and both head off into the afterlife. If someone is expelled from their village, heaven is no longer an option. They have to be buried at the place of their birth.

The islanders' clothes have to be seen to be believed. I encountered a mass of colours: pinks, yellows, whites, blues, and in every shade you can imagine. To bring back memories, I often pore over those vivid images in my photo album.

As you drive down any road, you'll see beautiful women on their way to the temples with their offerings. On their heads, they carry gigantic baskets full of fruit and flowers. The baskets also contain nuts and rice cakes in a multiplicity of colours.

On the ground outside every house, small bamboo baskets are set down containing items such as rice, flowers and incense sticks. These are offerings for the gods, intended to bring prosperity, health or help with other important issues, and to ward off evil spirits. It's the job of the woman of the house to prepare these offerings.

Traditional beliefs are a cornerstone of Balinese society and the gods and demons are honoured almost everywhere you look. Earlier in this book, I referred to myself as a woman in two worlds. The Balinese also live in two worlds: the seen or conscious world is the 'sekala' and the unseen or spirit world is the 'niskal'.

If an islander's balance in both worlds needs adjusting, he or she can call on a 'balian', a traditional healer. The balian's job is to help the patients restore balance in both worlds. I'm interested in alternative medicine and therapies, and I find the balians' techniques fascinating. For example, if you have a cold, a healer will cover your chest in tiger balm and then scrape you with a coin until the skin is red. It gets rid of some of your skin, and your cold disappears too.

If a family is going through a troubled time, ancestors could be to blame. The islanders believe their forebears can cause mischief and real harm if not treated regularly to their favourite treats and offerings. The balian may go into a trance to discover what the problem is. The patient can receive plant medicine, or sometimes a massage will do the trick. His tools come from the lush landscape, which provides a herbal medicine called jamu.

I mentioned earlier that the religion derives from Hinduism. However, it incorporates many more ideas, delving far into the past. The original islanders believed in animism, and you can see and feel the effects there today. The idea is that a spiritual realm exists alongside humans. Believers say that humans possess souls, and that souls have life apart from their bodies before and after death. A soul or spirit also exists in every object, even if it's inanimate, such as a rock or tree. This is one of man's oldest beliefs and is thought to go back to the Stone Age.

Stones and trees are believed to be the homes of invisible beings. You'll see small shrines or temples alongside them. Every rice paddy has a temple and you'll find them at crossroads, graveyards and rivers. The local villagers prepare small offerings and leave them in bamboo baskets on and around the stone or tree. Bali is sometimes known as the Island of the Gods, or the Island of Ten Thousand Temples. Yes, I would say there could be that many, as every village has its collection of them.

Pura Besakih is the island's 'mother' temple, and it's built on the southern face of the 'mother' mountain, Gunung Agung. Pura Ulun Danu is the water temple at Lake Aanau Bratan. I think it's the most beautiful of all the temples in Bali. Then there's the sunset temple, Tanah Lot, a wonderful sight with the sun setting behind it. It's usually surrounded by water, but you can walk up to it at low tide. No one is allowed inside apart from a select few.

The Balinese are terrified of witchcraft. Those who practise black and white magic can either harm or heal. That's why household offerings are made to the spirits, to keep them content. If black magic prevails, a village can fall into danger, and that's when purification ceremonies are carried out to restore a proper equilibrium.

The Rice Goddess, Dewa Sri, is honoured in the fields. She's a fertility symbol and you'll see miniature statues of her on sale. She's usually holding fertile eggs, rice, animals or birds. Tradition dictates that, when the daily meal has been cooked, tiny rice offerings must be set out before food can be consumed.

Another key aspect of family life is the way children are named. The Balinese have no problems finding names for their newborn children. There are only four first names to choose from. The first-born is called Wayan; number two is called Made; the third child is called Nyoman; and the fourth goes by the name of Ketut. When child number five comes along, you start again with Wayan.

For travellers to Bali, it can be confusing trying to keep track of all the Ketuts and Wayans. Families themselves give nicknames to children to help keep tabs on everyone.

Back on the tourist trail, I must mention the Bali Museum. It's in Denpasar and houses the world's finest collection of Balinese art. The exhibits there affected me so much I felt like I was in a trance for days. The items on show are out of this world, as are the buildings and their settings. The exterior walls, gates and courtyards give the impression of being in a royal palace. There are carved doors, stone sculptures and the centrepiece is an enormous, ornate ceremonial gate. History buffs can enjoy looking at relics dating from the Bronze Age to the 19th century. It's an astonishing place.

Even before the terrorist bombings, poverty was rife on the island. In the mountain areas, thousands of people have literally nothing. Many have no water, sanitation, roads, schools, health facilities or electricity. I discovered that illiteracy in some parts is almost 100 per cent.

Malnutrition is a growing problem in places, along with iodine deficiency disorders. Iodine is an essential nutrient for healthy childbirth, as well as for body and brain development. Several charities are trying their best to help, but from my recollection there's a long way to go.

My first trip to the supermarket brought a few surprises. I saw local people buying packets of a white substance, and I assumed it was sugar. But no, it was monosodium glutamate, or msg, in huge doses. Because the people are poor, their food, and meat in particular, tends to be of low quality, so they use msg to boost the flavours.

When I was on holiday in Bali, before settling there, we stayed with our friend Steve, who has a garment-export business. I actually met him in Sweden when I was studying, before I knew T, and we became very close friends. Steve moved to Bali and fell in love with the place. When he came to England, he stayed with us and talked about business opportunities in Bali. T's ears pricked up when he heard about the island's potential. Steve and T got on like a house on fire, and they became firm friends even before our Bali adventure.

Of all the mistakes I've made in my life – and there have been a few – one really stands out above the rest. I just wanted some cash of my own, not to be controlled financially. I'm an independent woman, after all. Maybe that streak in me – not my highlights, although I wanted those too – made me rebel against the situation.

My mother wanted to send some money to her children, as all parents do. For me, that worked out at $2,000 and I thought I could use my newfound wealth for a project. But I wanted to hide the transaction from T. Steve agreed that my mother should transfer the money into his account in Bali. The money came, and Steve gave me the cash.

I met a French football coach called Alain and the two of us discussed a business venture. Alain suggested that we could make some money. The idea was to pay for a container back to France, with traditional teak Bali furniture and other items inside. His mother ran a furniture shop in France and the potential mark-up was enormous.

T saw me chatting to Alain and became suspicious. He thought we were having an affair or something. Well, Alain was a handsome Frenchman, but nothing like that entered my mind. We were having a furtive chat about our business plan. I reckon T was jealous of Alain because he got on well with the boys, playing jokes and having fun with them.

I decided to tell T what I was up to and how I hoped to make a decent profit from the container scheme. I hadn't kept anything from him before, but this time I should have kept my mouth firmly shut. T went ballistic. Because he always needed to be in control, he was furious that he'd been left out of this particular transaction.

The reason I didn't tell him was that he never gave me any money. I thought, if I told him what I was up to, he'd demand the money for the business. I wanted it for myself;

I didn't want to keep asking him for money. I thought, if I could build up my own finances, I'd feel more secure.

T demanded Alain's telephone number and gave him such a roasting that, inside my head, I can still hear him ranting. No wonder Alain cooled on the project, left the island and gave me some of the money back. I did make a small loss on the project. He wanted nothing more to do with me, T or any container scheme, so I could hardly blame him.

I hadn't heard the last of the container fiasco. In 2000, we had some friends with us in Bali to celebrate the Millennium. While they were staying with us, we went on a trip to a small island off Bali.

T acted most oddly during that holiday. He sat on the beach on his own and kept avoiding me. One night he woke me up in the middle of the night. He said he had something to tell me. 'Because of this business with Alain, I went and had an affair,' he confessed. 'I know it was wrong, and I'm really sorry. Please can we forget about both incidents?'

'Hang on a minute,' I said. 'I didn't have an affair with Alain or anyone else. I liked him, but it was strictly business. You can't compare that to you going off and having sex with another woman.'

I was feeling hurt and shocked, but I said I would forgive him on the condition that we dropped the subject completely. After all, it was the Millennium and a fresh start seemed to be in order.

Later, in the English court, T's affidavit started with the container story, and how he was convinced that I'd had an affair. Well, we'd agreed not to go there, so I was confused that the story about Alain was emerging as a big issue. I'd understood that the container episode was dead and buried.

I know that T has never forgiven me for trying to put my business plan into action, and not telling him about it. I should have revealed my scheme, I know, but I felt I had to keep it quiet at the time.

To add to my woes in Bali, I received grim news from Denmark. My brother called to say that my father had died, aged 86. At first, I was stunned, and it just deepened my misery. But I tried to think that he'd lived to a ripe old age, and had enjoyed having a very late child (me) at the age of 50. We had shared so many good times, though, and I was so sad.

I assumed that we would all be going home for the funeral. However, T said that wasn't possible, and I felt he was cold about the whole affair. 'My sister and my brother never came to my father's funeral,' he told me. 'Why is it so important for you to go? He's dead, there's nothing you can do.'

'OK, if you can't come, then I'll go on my own for a few days,' I said.

'Who's going to look after the children?' T argued. 'I have a business to look after. Do you expect me to be a babysitter?'

'OK, I'll take all the children with me. It's not a problem,' I replied.

'Who's going to pay for all those tickets?' he countered. 'Do you expect me to pay? I'm not paying for all those tickets. Are you crazy?'

Financially, I knew that the air fares would not have been a problem. But we didn't go, and that was that.

I wrote a speech for my uncle, and it was read out in church. I arranged to have a flower arrangement made for my dad's coffin. I was so upset that I couldn't attend his funeral. I found it unbelievable that we couldn't go. Anyway, my dad's final chapter closed and I moved on to the next one in my life. And it could have finished me for good.

T and I were going through another crisis in Bali, through a time when I wasn't sleeping properly, and a friend gave me some sleeping tablets. I'd never taken sleeping tablets before; these turned out to be super-strength knockout drops.

Early one evening, I felt I couldn't take any more. I cooked T's dinner. The children had already eaten. Adam was with one of the maids, on walkabout in the village. The three other boys were outside playing.

I left T's meal for him and felt I had to go out. I grabbed my bag containing the tablets. I felt I was the loneliest, most miserable person on earth. T had been so cold. I felt I deserved a lot better.

I headed off on my pushbike – a second-hand acquisition which served me well – and thought I would make for the coast. The nearest beach was quite deserted, because it was too dangerous to swim. Anyway, that's where I decided to go.

I cycled the mile or so to the beach, hardly meeting a living soul, past rice paddies. I didn't feel as if I belonged there at all. It was a beautiful place, though, and the air was warm. The sun was just setting and, although I could see beauty all around me, I could feel nothing but sadness.

I left my bike at the end of the road leading to the beach. I took my shoes off and walked down towards the water and sat beneath a palm tree. As I reached into my bag, my hand nudged those tablets. Don't ask me why, but as I gazed at the extraordinary sunset I took four of them out and gulped them down.

The only thing I remember was a sensation of drowning. I'd fallen into a deep sleep by the edge of the sea. The tide crept in, with me still out for the count, having taken four of the strongest sleeping pills ever made.

As time went by, the maid became worried about me and called my friend Djati (my regular rescuer) from the house phone. He rounded up a search party of local lads on motorbikes and they began to scour the area. They went down to the beach and discovered my bike – minus me, of course.

I was still unconscious when they found me, with the water starting to lap around my legs. Two of the boys carried me to one of the bikes. I was sandwiched between Djati, who drove, and one of the boys as a makeshift method of getting back home. Djati helped to carry me upstairs once we got there, and they put me to bed.

The next thing I remember was waking up and seeing T standing over me, looking angry and irritated, with his arms crossed. I felt heavy-headed and had a huge painful burn on the inside of my leg. That came from dangling over the motorbike engine.

T glared at me and asked gruffly, 'Do you want to go to England or Denmark? You need to get away from me and the children.' He stomped off.

I never told T what had happened. He later said in an affidavit in the English court that I often came home drunk in Bali and had to be put in bed by the maids, and was generally an unfit mother. Thank God that Djati saved my life so that I could prove to be a worthy individual, after all.

Earlier, I mentioned the Bali bomb of 2002 and how lucky I was to get out of there before that tragic event. After I left, it preyed on my mind a lot. I had many good friends on the island.

I made a few enquiries to found out how everyone I knew had been affected. Well, immediately after the 2002 blast, hotel bookings fell by 80 per cent. But the entire island pulled together to get its image back.

After about three years, tourists were returning and most foreigners thought the explosion must have been a one-off. Gradually, the hotels filled up and the future looked promising for such a fragile tourism industry.

All their hard work was undone when bombers struck again in October 2005. My friend Steve had two shops in Bali, so he took a double whammy. The explosions had a devastating effect on his business.

I read in the newspapers that some holidaymakers on the island at the time of the 2005 bomb insisted on completing their stay. Many said they wouldn't be put off and would return in future years. I saw one woman tell a reporter that, if everyone left, the islanders would have nothing. Another holidaymaker said he was encouraged by the new heightened security.

At the time of writing the tourists have returned. Steve called me to say business was booming again and he'd bought a new Mercedes.

I pray for the people of Bali.

9

A BRIEF ROMANCE

The plane from Bali to England was my time for reflection. I reflected on the loss of my children. I also remembered George. I hadn't looked for romance in Bali, but it came along and found me. I closed my eyes and thought about George for a while.

During the days after T left, I vowed never again to get involved in that type of a relationship. I made a promise to myself and I intended to keep it. I promised that if I became involved with anyone he'd be non-possessive and fun to be with. I wasn't going to play the dutiful wife again.

My self-esteem was very low. I know I probably looked all right, but I felt old and unattractive. Looking back, I realise I still had my figure, my blonde hair and my other attributes. I just didn't see it at the time.

Overwhelmed by my miserable situation, I had no thoughts of men whatsoever. I was dealing with nice men all the time, but I just saw them as people. All I thought about was the children, if they were happy, if they thought about me, and why all this was happening to me.

All that changed about four months after T left. I was out having lunch at a Greek restaurant with my friend Anne, another teacher. We sat discussing the English School Bali and its mounting problems. I was trying to run everything on my own. Parents weren't too impressed that the school's owner had disappeared with his four children. I spent a lot of time persuading parents that they should stick with the school, despite the recent drama.

I told Anne I believed I could keep everything going and I was committed to the staff and the pupils. She was on my side, reassuring me that the teachers would give me their full backing. Those were the words I wanted to hear, as my stress levels were going off the scale. What was about to happen next also pushed other levels, the ones only a woman knows about, to new limits.

Out of the corner of my eye, I could see a tall, blond, good-looking man sitting opposite a woman. I tried to make out if she was his girlfriend. They didn't appear intimate and I couldn't detect any chemistry. Their table was only three feet away and I was attracted to his laugh. They were chatting happily, but I got the impression that she was perhaps a colleague. Just listening to that laugh cheered me up no end.

I thought I'd better keep talking to Anne in case he saw me looking. 'This may not be politically correct,' I told her. 'But if I have another relationship the man will be whiter than white. I don't want to become involved with anyone who has Arab connections. I don't know who the man will be, but those are my ground rules.'

Anne laughed out loud and told me I couldn't be that fussy. I reminded her about what had happened, and so I was going to be the fussiest woman in history.

Certainly the jolly figure in the corner of my eye seemed to fit the bill. As I talked to Anne, half looking at him, I could see he was also glancing over at me. I felt flattered by his attention and a little spark ignited inside me; I'd been stifled for so long that I didn't realise the spark existed.

It felt so good, realising that someone seemed to be admiring me. What was he looking at? My hair? My face? Maybe he liked the skirt I was wearing, and my legs. I wasn't sure, but I needed to find out. Maybe he would be attracted to my Danish background, or perhaps he would be interested to know that I'd learned about acupuncture. All those facts assembled in my head at once, so for a few seconds my emotions all came together and created a muddle inside my brain.

When I glanced over again, he was still looking at me. All of a sudden, I felt hot and my mouth went dry. We'd only exchanged glances, but I wanted to get to know him. I wondered if I looked sexy, after all I'd been through. I felt the urge to paint my fingernails, toenails, show off my figure and put on my best strappy heels and a nice dress. My heart raced as these thoughts filled my head.

A surfing record came on the restaurant's crackly radio and I pictured myself driving down to the beach with him in an open-topped car. I felt like a naughty teenager. I began to have silly thoughts. I began to shuffle across the seat to show my brown legs, at the same time thinking, Don't be such a tart, Helle! I scanned the restaurant nervously, as I didn't want anyone else to get the wrong impression. A waiter stared at my legs, so reluctantly I eased them back under the table. When he wasn't looking, I revealed them again. How ridiculous, looking back, but that's what I did!

As I continued the conversation about the school, I knew I wouldn't be making much sense to Anne. I did manage to regain my concentration for a few minutes, but I started to quiver as I glanced across and realised he was still looking at me.

I felt so downcast when he left, and thought to myself, Hey, Helle, it's exciting that you can still have these emotions. You haven't had those feelings for a long time, girl.

If I was hot before he left, I was like a furnace when he reappeared on his own 20 minutes later. He walked through the door of the restaurant and came straight over to our table. His long, blond hair danced in the light of the candles as he strode across, and he had a great big smile on his face.

'Hi, I'm George,' he said in a strong South African accent. 'Can I buy you two ladies a drink?'

'Yes, please,' we chorused, and I concentrated on not having any more of those hot flushes. Although my face was tanned, I had the feeling that if my temperature rose any more I'd look like a beetroot.

George went up to the bar and ordered glasses of ouzo for us, and all the time I was thinking about how gorgeous he looked. He returned with the drinks, and confirmed that he was indeed South African and that he was working for a property developer in Bali.

As George described the various jobs he was involved in, I became more and more excited, and my emotions were well and truly stirred. He said he was 26. I told him I was 36, just to get it out of the way, but he didn't make any comment. He just looked at me and said, 'No way, you look far too young. You don't look a day over 30.'

It was no coincidence that the conversation moved into what I was going to do with my house: sell it or rent it out. I gave him my home and mobile numbers, praying that he wouldn't just call me about my future plans for the villa. I accidentally, on purpose maybe, brushed my leg against his but he didn't seem to notice.

I felt dejected when he left again. However, I had him in the back of my mind as a pleasant alternative to my present situation. When I thought about our first meeting, it cheered me up. I realised I hadn't laughed so much for ages.

My mind seemed to be divided into several sections. The main part thought about my kids all the time; another part thought about the school finances, off and on; and this new area featuring George was an interesting development. When I pictured him, I felt happier, so I tried to picture him as much as I could.

The fantastic, tall, blond South African with the infectious laugh didn't call that day. He didn't call the next day either, or the next. Soon five days had gone by. I had been really hoping he'd call me, but when I heard nothing I tried to put this imaginary affair to the back of my mind.

With my hopes well and truly dashed, I continued working as normal at the school. One day, between classes, I nipped out to the bank to see if I could appease them, and when I returned the secretary handed me a card. It was a beautiful arty card, covered with flowers.

Inside, George had written, 'Dear Helle, I'm so sorry I haven't called you. The day after I met you at the restaurant, I lost my phone and your number. I remembered that you owned the English School Bali, so I knew where to find you. Here's my number. Please call me.'

My hot flush returned with a vengeance, and I was cooking from the very end of my natural blonde hair to the end of my newly painted toenails. I could feel myself shaking as I read the card over and over again. I'd become in the past such a dutiful wife that these emotions felt new and fresh to me.

By now, I knew I was looking good. I'd been for a manicure, a pedicure and any other cures within my budget. I was nervous about calling George. I wished he hadn't lost my number. I wanted him to call me. I fancied him and wanted to see him, but I felt awkward having to make the call, so I decided to sleep on it.

When I woke up the next day, I opened my handbag and read the card again. I worked on my courage and by the afternoon I had plucked up enough of the stuff to make the call. I rang his home number, but there was no reply. I was relieved for a minute and I thought that maybe he would see my number and ring me instead. Reality kicked in, and I knew I was being silly, so I called his mobile number.

His mobile rang for what seemed like a full minute, then he answered.

'Hi,' I whispered in what must have sounded like a meek little voice. 'It's Helle.'

'Helle, Helle.' His strong accent came through straight away. 'Hey, thanks so much for calling. I'm so sorry I lost your number. I'm really, really pleased that you've called.'

I felt at ease straight away. George suggested that we meet for a drink and a bite to eat around eight o'clock. I agreed instantly.

I knew that all this attention was the best thing for me right now, because it gave me some extra zest. I started to get ready; not nervous any more, just wondering how the evening would go.

I ran a bath and poured in my favourite oils. It felt like I spent hours doing my hair and make-up. I wanted to get it just right. Then I tried on outfit after outfit, top after top. To my horror I realised they were all old, from my dismal married days, and put them in a plastic bag. I did have a nice dress, which showed off my figure, but he'd already seen that one in the Greek restaurant.

I checked the time and thought I might just make it to a clothes shop. On the way there, I stopped my car and dumped the plastic bag containing my old clothes in a dustbin. It was like shedding an old skin.

By now, it was six o'clock. I parked and raced from shop to shop, trying to find the right outfit. By seven, I'd tried dresses with a split, without a split, some too revealing, others too tight. At last, I saw a short black dress; it fitted me perfectly and I headed back home, weaving a path through the tourist traffic. I thought I needed another shower, because it was so hot outside, but I was running out of time.

I rushed into Nattalia's house, put on the dress, touched up my make-up again and headed off into the sultry Balinese night. I was running late, but I knew he wouldn't stand me up. Anyway, I remembered from my single days that women were always late. I parked outside the restaurant. It was 8.15.

Wow! I saw an Adonis of a man, who oozed sex appeal, sitting at the bar. It was George. He was wearing casual jeans and a black T-shirt. Wow! again.

There was an instant spark. We chatted for ages about my situation, and I told him all about my kids and how they'd disappeared. He was genuinely interested. I liked that.

We chatted about anything and everything, and all the time I was wondering if I was doing the right thing. I didn't know if he was going to ask me to sleep with him; maybe he didn't want to sleep with me. My knees were knocking under my short skirt, and I thought he would hear them.

I had a slight panic attack while we chatted, because I hadn't slept with another man for ages. My relationship with T was strained for a long time, so I knew that proper sex would come as a shock to my system. As we enjoyed our first drink, he put his arm around me and I felt a rush of excitement. I thought I'd had too much wine, so I decided to leave the car and pick it up the next day.

George said he was OK to drive and produced the keys for his jeep. He ran me home to Nattalia's house, where I was staying. He leaned over to kiss me and I wasn't sure what to expect.

I didn't want him to come in for coffee, because it wasn't my place. His hand brushed my face and he touched my leg briefly. Then we kissed. He had beautiful soft lips, and deep down inside I felt a rush of passion. I knew I had to make a sharp exit to keep my emotions in check.

He asked me if I would meet him the next day, and I rapidly agreed. The thought of seeing him again made me perspire. I realised I was becoming a normal woman once more, and it felt brilliant.

I slid out of the car like a lump of jelly and tottered off, ungainly in my high heels. I was feeling a little apprehensive about telling anyone I was seeing George, because of my situation, so I kept it all to myself. I didn't even tell Nattalia, although I was keen to share my news with someone.

We met every evening for about a week, just chatting and watching the sunsets. The inevitable was looming. He invited me over to his place for a meal on the following Friday evening, and I wondered where that would lead.

He didn't actually cook a meal; we had a takeaway and ate it on his bed while we watched a movie. The fact that I was on his bed, wearing my new tight jeans and a new top meant that other events were certain to take place. My wardrobe had certainly expanded over the past week.

I wanted him and he wanted me. So far, there had been hardly any touching and I was nervous about having someone else in my life. When the movie finished, George leaned over, kissed me and undid my top.

That surge of passion I had felt in his jeep turned into a torrent. Although my husband had left me, I somehow felt I was being unfaithful. On the other hand, I was enjoying all this attention and I had to get this 'first time' out of the way.

He undressed me gently, and one touch led to another, then another. The touching became more and more intense, and soon we were making love. It was beautiful, and I cried. I didn't feel guilty at all. I hadn't had sex for a long time, and it was a sensational experience. I felt I was making a comeback as a healthy, youngish female.

It felt as if I was being reborn. We made love all night, and for several nights afterwards. He was so romantic. One evening he filled up his large bath and covered it with rose petals. He also poured in aromatic oils and as I lay there soaking up the atmosphere he joined me in the bath. We made love among the rose petals and the fragrant oils. What a contrast to my previous existence!

George and I never had an argument, and not one bad word passed between us. We phoned and texted each other all the time, and I couldn't wait to see him every day. The relationship gave me renewed energy; energy to work out how I was going to track down the children; to handle the school's finances; and to get away from my tropical island once and for all.

Deep down I knew it wasn't going to last. We had a ten-year age gap and he often went back to South Africa. Our meetings became less frequent as I worked on new ways to see the children. He knew that the kids were my life and, although I was very, very fond of him, the relationship was a bit of a diversion for me.

When it was time for him to leave for home, I didn't get too upset. The relationship had helped me a lot. George had been a good listener. He'd given me lots of encouragement. He'd brought out the woman in me.

The aircraft banked steeply as it soared into the paper-thin cloud over my tropical island. I'd dozed off for a few minutes and dreamed a little. As I looked down, the lush green landscape of Bali became a smaller and smaller dot.

Over the horizon, more drama would unfold in the coming months.

10

BACK IN ENGLAND

It was a long, lonely flight back to England. My mind kept going over my disastrous past few years; my recent most horrendous setback; the pleasant memory of George; and the challenges that lay ahead.

As I looked down from the aircraft, I wondered where my children were, who was looking after them and if they were missing their mum. The ocean sparkled and they even served sparkling wine on the plane. I was dead inside.

I arrived at Heathrow and there to meet me was my close friend Caroline. She'd driven up from her home in Romsey, near Southampton. We hadn't seen one another for three years, so it was an emotional reunion. We just hugged each other and I couldn't hold back the tears. I just cried and cried, thinking I would never stop.

We drove back to Caroline's house, where we talked things over for several days. I was so grateful that I could stay with Caroline and her partner. I don't know where else I could have stayed.

I was worried about staying too long there. Caroline had a big, busy job as a professor at Southampton University and her partner worked with computers. I didn't want to lumber them with my problems, although they were happy to discuss anything with me.

I tried not to feel too sorry for myself, but I was more than a little deflated. The only thing that kept me going was my telephone chats with the boys. They were staying with T's brother, Adnan, in Saudi. Adnan's wife, Alia, insisted that they should talk to me, so I thanked God for that.

There was a treat on the horizon, and I felt that I deserved it. Another very dear friend, Tracey, suggested a break in Barbados, but I thought she was winding me up. How could I afford a trip to Barbados? Well, Tracey worked for a major airline and flew all over the world. She was allowed to put several people on her concessions list, and that included yours truly.

Earlier, I mentioned the bombings in Bali. I actually found out about the 2002 atrocity when we arrived in Barbados. As soon as we reached the hotel, I logged on to the internet to check my e-mails. I was horrified to see pictures of the aftermath. What? I'd only just left the island and it had been the perfect picture of peace and harmony. Now it was thrown into chaos. My e-mail box was full from people, all over the world, wondering if I was all right. Of course, many of my friends assumed I was still there.

I called my boys from Barbados. We talked about what had happened in Bali. Little did I know that this was the last time I would speak to them for five months. Yes, five whole months. Nowadays, I'd find it hard not talking to them for a day; imagine how I felt during those five long months.

We did have a wonderful break in Barbados. Although it was hard to forget all my troubles and worries, we rented a car and saw the sights. We went out clubbing at night and I felt better about things until the next morning. It was like popping a tablet to take the edge off my woes, but they always returned with a vengeance.

I used Tracey as a sounding board for all my ideas and crazy schemes to see my children. Maybe I should hire private detectives and kidnap them back, I thought. That was just one of my nutty ideas. Tracey also soaked up all my tears in the mornings, when a night of drinking and clubbing had worn off.

As soon as I arrived back in England from Barbados, I tried to call the children. I spoke to T's brother, who told me that T and the boys had moved. He gave me a number, supposedly of the new house, but I couldn't get through. When I called T's brother back and said the number didn't work, he said to just keep trying. I found out later that T disconnected the phone when he wasn't using it.

About four days later, more bad news arrived in the post. My friend Caroline – who knew T from past times in England – received a letter from the man himself. I'd told the children I was going to stay with Caroline, so they must have told their father. I felt very unworthy again, not even fit to receive a letter myself.

T said I had to start divorce proceedings in the UK. He said that, once he had the divorce papers in his hand in Saudi, he'd let me speak to the children again. He also mentioned that he was getting married again, to a Saudi woman, and that the boys would have a stepmother. He told Caroline that everyone concerned in the arrangement was very happy. I presumed I was now omitted from the entire scenario.

I contacted a solicitor in Southampton and started the required divorce proceedings. I then contacted Reunite, who were helpful and sympathetic but had no real power to take action. They advised me to contact the Saudi Embassy in London, the Foreign Office and the British Embassy in Jeddah. One woman against a world of red tape, I thought.

The Saudi Embassy really didn't want to know. They kept passing me on to one office after another. However, after much perseverance, I managed to get an appointment with the vice consul in person.

The Foreign Office pointed out the difficulties of dealing with Saudi Arabia. They said the children, although British, had been abducted from Indonesia to Saudi Arabia, not from the UK to Saudi Arabia. I got the distinct impression they didn't want to know. They said they came across many similar cases and there was very little they could do. Take the matter up with the Indonesian authorities, they suggested. Thanks, guys.

Well, no one was going to get rid of me that easily. I decided to contact Abdullah Al-Johani, the Saudi lawyer I'd called from Bali. Abdullah sounded polite and switched on, just as during my first telephone call to him. He explained how difficult it was to actually get into the country. He told me all about visas and how tricky they were to arrange. The odds were stacked heavily against me, he said, but he would help me fight my battle. I sent off his initial fee to get the ball rolling.

I continued with a barrage of daily telephone calls. I spoke to the main man at the British Consulate in Jeddah. He went on at some length, explaining that there was little they could do to help me. I made it very clear that I wasn't likely to give up my children. I said I didn't accept that nothing could be done about the situation.

'Whether you like it or not, I'm not going to go away,' I told him firmly. 'I'll be trying to get my children back every hour of every day.' I meant it. I was on the case full-time.

About a week later, Abdullah contacted me to say he'd located T and the children. They were living in a rented house in Jeddah and T was operating an acupuncture clinic in the building.

Abdullah also had the name of the children's school. It was an international school, thank God. I found it on the internet and discovered that – as well as teaching Arabic and Islam – it followed part of the British curriculum. What a relief that the boys weren't attending a Saudi school. I discovered later that they had attended a Saudi school for a short time, but it was a complete waste of time as they didn't speak any Arabic.

My meeting at the Saudi Embassy went well. They were certainly understanding and I got the impression that they had several similar cases on their books. I could also see that being reunited with my boys in Saudi Arabia was a long shot.

I needed a visa to get into the country. It was going to be even more complicated for me, a single woman. I needed a sponsor, a maharam. This person must be a woman's husband, son, brother, father, or uncle or other blood relative. When a Saudi woman marries, her husband automatically becomes her maharam. But now, as T had divorced me under Saudi law, I was seen as a single woman there. I had no say in this. He could divorce me, and have several other wives if he wished.

A pleasant-sounding Egyptian man from the Saudi Embassy was dealing with my case. He promised he would do his best to get me a visiting visa as soon as possible. I went away from my first meeting with him feeling positive and ready to pack my suitcase. I had no idea that it would be another eight months before I received my visa.

I was still staying with Caroline. She very kindly put up with me and was the rock I could lean against when it all became too overwhelming. Her family helped me to keep my head and emotions together.

Around the beginning of November 2002, I took a full-time job as a receptionist with a wine-importing company in Romsey. This helped me to take my mind off my problems and the constant pain of missing my children. While I was working there, I met a poet. He wrote about my plight in words that touched me so much, I still carry them around in my handbag:

I see shadows
I see Helle
I see dust on bottles
Dust in the cellar
Perhaps depths of despair
She has visited there
And her story, now it's told
Where is the street
Paved with gold?
Another man; another land
Could he ever understand?

Evil days and evil nights
Yet truth survives
Burning bright
An awesome power
To quash the lie
The candle flickers
But can never die.

My Christmas present that year didn't come wrapped. No one gave it to me. It wasn't really a present at all, but it surpassed anything I'd ever received at Christmas.

Just before the big day, I was feeling lower than ever, missing the children terribly and furious that I wasn't allowed to talk to them. I worked out that the last time I'd heard their voices was during that holiday in Barbados.

I sat there in my office, looking at my mobile phone, and I somehow had the urge to call T's brother in Jeddah. I thought Uncle Adnan might tell me how the kids were getting on, as I had no way of reaching T for the information.

Someone answered straight away. 'Hello,' said a young, familiar-sounding voice. I froze. It was my six-year-old, Adam. I laughed, then I wept, all in a few seconds, and I didn't know what to say. I wondered whether I should speak at all, in case he got into trouble.

'Is that Adam?' I asked, praying that the voice at the other end belonged to my son.

'Yes, it's Adam,' said the tiny voice, thousands of miles away but as if he were standing next to me.

I knew I had to say a lot of things very quickly, as the line could go dead at any time. I remember cramming in what I could, speaking at about twice my normal speed. I guessed that T and the boys were visiting his brother, so I had to make the most of every second.

'Adam, it's Mummy. How are you? I miss you so much, my darling. I love you so much. I'm trying everything to come to see you. How are your brothers? Would you like me to come to see you?'

'Mummy, I love you too,' Adam answered. 'I have a stepmum now, and Baba [Dad] says I have to call her "Mum". Where are you, Mummy? Maybe it's best that you don't come now, because Baba's going to be angry. I can't talk. Someone is coming and I have to go.'

He put the phone down and I had that totally desolate feeling again. I started to cry as it sank in that Adam was having to call his stepmum 'Mum'. I kicked the desk. I wanted my babies back. At the same time, I was relieved he'd put down the receiver to avoid any trouble.

I spent Christmas Day 2002 with Caroline, her daughter and partner Steve. The memory of talking to my young son Adam on the phone meant that was all I could think about. I washed their two cars and my own to take my mind off the telephone call.

God, I was miserable, thinking about all the children all over the world opening their presents on Christmas morning. Mine were cooped up in a house in the desert where they didn't even celebrate Christmas. I knew that no presents were being given out and no one would be wished a Happy Christmas.

I would have spent all my savings just to say 'Merry Christmas' to my boys. I guess the festive season is the worst time for left-behind mums.

After six months, I felt I was imposing on Caroline and

her family. They wanted to look after me, but I felt I needed to move away to give them a break. My friend John, the faith healer from Bali, called me because he'd returned to England. He was renting a large house in Canterbury and looking for someone to share with.

John has an English degree and a particular skill in writing letters. He helped me to phrase exactly my sentiments in the letters I sent to all and sundry, including Saudi princes, lawyers, government officials and a few more besides.

We stayed in a town house called the Apple Store, a quaint old building. It had traditional beams and yet was modern inside. I could sense its colourful history as a destination for produce from the local orchards.

We went on day trips through the 'Garden of England' and I discovered parts of the country that I didn't know existed. I was fascinated by odd-looking buildings shaped like ice-cream cones. I had a look inside one which had been converted into a B&B. The owner told me that hops, for brewing, were dried out over blankets of horsehairs. The conical roof apparently created a good draught for the fire. In recent years, these distinctive oast houses have fallen into disuse because of the growing trade in imported hops.

I sought solace at an even older attraction, Leeds Castle near Maidstone. It's been described as 'the loveliest castle in the world' and it looks that way, sitting in 500 acres of splendid grounds. I gazed at the majestic architecture, surrounded by the customary moat, and wished my sons were with me for the day out. I knew they'd have enjoyed seeing the one hundred species of endangered birds and the museum, but I soaked up the atmosphere alone.

On the job front, I'd left the wine importers and become a temp in Canterbury at £5 an hour. I think I may just have scraped the minimum wage, but it was the only work I could find at that time. I also took another part-time job at a hotel, organising weddings in the local countryside.

When there were no weddings, I tackled the housekeeping and cooking. Having four boys is an expensive business, especially when you're saving up to free them from an ordeal thousands of miles away.

Most of my friends were still in the Southampton area, so I travelled over there quite a lot to see them. Around this time, I also met David, a television journalist, who told me that I should write down all my experiences as it would make a fascinating book. 'Keep notes of everything,' he advised. 'I've covered hundreds of stories in my time, but yours takes the biscuit. I bet there's lots more to come too.'

Being Danish, I had to get him to explain the bit about the biscuit. And he was right: there was an awful lot more to come.

David told his company, Meridian Broadcasting, about me and they carried several items about my case. Other journalists picked up the story and soon I was headline news. It was strange seeing myself on television and in magazines.

Perhaps this media coverage helped me. I had several more meetings with the man from the Saudi Embassy, who was charming and seemed very sympathetic towards me. However, the big stumbling block continued to get in the way. As I mentioned earlier, I needed a visa – and for the visa I needed that male sponsor, the maharam. Now, how was I going to get round that one?

Well, I must say the Saudis were most helpful at this stage. They contacted T and both his brothers and told them a visa could be issued on their verbal agreement. I reckon they were keen to get rid of me and get the case resolved in a positive way.

That route was a dead end: T said he didn't want me in Saudi Arabia, and his brothers didn't want to get involved.

I felt I was never going to see the children. I couldn't talk to them. I didn't know if they were receiving the presents I'd sent to his brother's address, nor if they realised how much I loved them and how hard I was trying to see them. I plunged into even deeper despair.

Now I was beginning to panic. My normal cool manner had left me. I thought I should increase my knowledge of Saudi Arabia. I studied maps, history books, geography books, everything I could find.

I gained bundles of inspiration from Betty Mahmoody's book *Not Without My Daughter*. I could see similarities emerging. Her husband had gone to his homeland, Iran, another hard-line Muslim country. He had become an entirely different person: he screamed at her, mistreated her terribly and took her daughter away. I could see a common theme running through all this. I rented the film, starring Sally Field, and began to hate Betty's husband as much as I hated mine.

I also kept writing letters to HRH Prince Turki Al-Faisal, the then Saudi Ambassador to the UK. The fact that he was the brother of the late King of Saudi Arabia had no bearing on the matter, of course! I didn't receive a reply from him.

Time was moving on and by the start of May 2003 I felt

lower than ever before. I'd written endless letters, e-mails and faxes to the Foreign Office, the Saudi Embassy and anyone else who might be able to help me.

Zak's tenth birthday was on 4 May. I couldn't get my head around not even talking to him on his big day.

Then something unexpected happened. The day after his birthday, I logged into my computer. I hadn't checked my e-mails for a few days and, oh, how I regretted that. There, in my inbox, was a message from T. He'd sent me an e-mail saying that, if I wanted to talk to Zak on his birthday, I could call his brother's house at an exact time that morning. I felt physically sick. I called anyway and eventually spoke to Uncle Adnan. He said the children had been waiting to speak to me, but were now gone and wouldn't be back for several weeks. I had completely, totally and utterly missed the boat.

A few days later, I received an e-mail from T saying that I could call the children at Adnan's house every Friday afternoon. I took full advantage of that weekly arrangement, and in truth my life revolved around those precious minutes. I made up for five months of zero contact.

The calls made me even more determined to see the boys. I had nothing to lose. I decided to chase up the Saudi Embassy and asked to speak directly to Prince Turki Al-Faisal. With a name like that, I suspected he wouldn't take any calls, and I was right. I was put through to his secretary. She sounded rather grumpy as I explained my case and said I'd written letter after letter, sent fax after fax and e-mail after e-mail. I'd sent the letters by recorded delivery, so I knew they'd been received. The charming lady said it might be an idea if I sent all the letters again, by fax. Why I was having to do this I had no idea, but off I went to find a fax machine and kept it busy for most of the morning.

Once my work was done, I called her back and asked if everything had been received.

'I believe it's all here,' was the reply and, with a surprising touch of humour, 'but you've used up all of our fax paper!'

Then I played my trump card. I said that, if I didn't get a response to my letters by the next day, they would find me chained to the railings outside the Embassy. I would tell everyone my story; how my children had been abducted to Saudi Arabia; how I couldn't see them because of Saudi law; and, although the Embassy people had been friendly and helpful, I remained stuck in England with no visa.

She could tell I was serious. For my children, I would walk barefoot through the desert in the ferocious heat. And it almost came to that, as you'll discover later.

The next morning, the friendly Egyptian at the Embassy called an important meeting to say that a big meeting was taking place there to discuss my case. He said he would ring back as soon as he knew anything. I called the various reporters who were following my case and filled them in with the details.

A couple of hours later, my contact at the Embassy called again to say that HRH Prince Turki Al-Faisal had decided to sponsor me. It was to be a one-off, visiting visa for one month. He asked me to come to the Embassy with my passport the next day to collect the document.

The following day, as I clutched that precious gift in my hand, he told me sternly, 'Helle, I have a message from the Prince, who is now your sponsor. It says that when you get to Saudi Arabia you must follow Saudi law. You will not make trouble. You will cover your hair and you will look down when you walk past a male. This is a one-off visa. After this, we will not issue any more visas under these terms.'

Hey, I could cope with that. I was going to see my children.

God save the Prince!

11

SEARCH IN THE DESERT

I felt as if the Prince had saved my life. I could hardly believe it was true. I had a visa. I danced down Park Lane with my friend Leila. I held on to my bag, as if it contained a crock of gold. No way was I going to let go of my passport, with that all-important visa inside it.

Leila took me to an Islamic clothes shop to buy an abaya. Now, this isn't the height of fashion. It's a long black, opaque overcoat designed to hide any femininity and must be worn by all Saudi women in public places. You hang it by the front door and put it on over your clothes when you go out.

'Hey, Helle, where's your sex appeal gone?' she grinned mischievously. 'You had some before you came in here and it seems to have ... er ... em ... vanished.'

A glance in the mirror confirmed my worst fears: the outfit was hideous. Leila could see I hated it with a vengeance and her grin developed into a gentle, non-stop chuckle.

I could see the funny side, but it was no laughing matter. 'I know this is the most horrible outfit I've ever seen,' I told her as I scowled in the mirror. 'There's a chance, just a chance, that it'll help me to see the boys again. I'll wear it day and night for the rest of my life if it means I can see my children again.'

'That's just the start of it,' Leila said in a more serious tone as she flicked through a range of dull and dismal outfits. 'Just wait until you get out there, and see what else you have to wear.'

'They're not that bad,' I replied, trying to convince myself as I disappeared inside another abaya. Although it was in the standard black, this abaya had a brown floral strip down the front. I decided that was the one for me and I picked out a matching black scarf. On the down side, I was transformed from size eight to eighteen in an instant.

The shop assistant packed my purchases neatly into bags, and Leila and I headed off into the night to celebrate with a meal at a Lebanese restaurant not far from the Saudi Embassy. We said our farewells and I headed back to Canterbury with my essential new purchases.

I was getting excited. I knew I'd be flying out about a week later. I could hardly contain myself. I spent my time getting presents for the boys. I was on the telly again. ITV sent another reporter to see me and I gave them an interview about my forthcoming trip to Saudi. They gave me a video camera to take with me, but as things turned out I wasn't allowed to use it. I promised to update them during my trip.

I flew out from Heathrow in June 2003. Reporters met me at the airport and filmed my departure. It also meant some free publicity for the airline, who looked after me, gave me coffee and provided VIP treatment.

I was nervous throughout the journey. I'd sent a fax to Uncle Adnan to let the family know I was coming, and that I expected to spend time with my children. I'd also told the boys I was coming. However, I had no idea how or when I was going to see them.

We had a four-hour stop in the United Arab Emirates. The splendour and wealth of the Middle East came home to me as I made my way through the amazingly decorated VIP lounge. An array of exotic snacks greeted me and I munched my way through them as I worked out my future plans. I glanced at some literature about Saudi Arabia; it made grim reading and for the first time I felt frightened.

As we took off for Jeddah, the sky was a vivid blue without a fluff of cloud. Below I could see desert, but nothing else. Two hours later, the picture outside hadn't changed, and for a few minutes I longed for England's green fields. Then my mind was filled again with images of the children, and with their voices.

I had another look through my Saudi handbook. I knew it was vital to be correctly dressed, so I couldn't afford even the slightest mistake. The woman sitting next to me started to sort through her clothes and I reckoned I could pick up a few tips.

'Excuse me,' I ventured, wishing I'd talked to her during the flight instead of studying the sky and the desert. 'Do you mind if I watch you fixing your clothes?'

I was addressing a tiny woman of about 40 and I tried to work out if she was a Saudi citizen, or a visitor like me. She didn't speak, but understood what I said. I asked her if I was underdressed, because she was almost completely covered up in black. She even wore black gloves and black socks. I didn't like the look of those one little bit.

Beneath the woman's veil, I could see brown darting eyes with lots of make-up around them. I noticed from looking around the plane that the other women were getting ready, and I was pleased to see that make-up was allowed. The woman next to me still didn't speak but she smiled, leaned over and helped to fit my abaya. When I put on my black headscarf, she checked that no hair was showing. My seatbelt clicked into place. I was ready to enter Saudi Arabia.

I sat completely still, as the engine note changed and I felt the aircraft turn towards Jeddah. Then the runway came into view. The wheels bounced and touched down, and I could see the enormous terminal that was my next port of call.

The silent woman had a few words for me, after all. 'Forty-two degrees,' she whispered, without changing expression or even moving her lips much. 'I hope you have success with your visit.'

She was right about the temperature, and maybe it was even hotter. When the stewardess opened the door, a surge of heat flowed through the aircraft. I climbed down the stairs, feeling ungainly and wobbly, trying to hold all my bags. My abaya seemed too long and I almost toppled unceremoniously on to the tarmac.

I made a dash for the terminal and its air conditioning. I wanted to ask my fellow passenger, now she'd broken her silence, what she meant about me having success. I thought for a minute and it dawned on me that I was the odd one out on the plane. She seemed to know that I was on a mission, but that brief chat was our last, and she disappeared inside the vast building.

I felt vulnerable. The crowd rushed over to a desk where landing cards had to be filled in. I thought they'd have given me one on the plane; now I was jostling for position, trying to find a card and fill it in, but I couldn't find a pen. I snatched one from the table before anyone else could reach it, and went into full panic mode as I jotted down my details.

My stomach hurt badly. I knew it was nerves; it felt like a huge knot and, whatever I did, however I breathed, it wouldn't go away. I was also praying for a miracle: as I'd faxed T's brother about my arrival, I had the faint hope that the children would be waiting for me at the airport.

I joined the line for Immigration. It moved quickly and I was pleased about that. 'Everything's going to be absolutely fine,' I kept telling myself. Everyone seemed to have the correct papers and they were waved through one by one. I relaxed for a second as I thought I would also go straight through. No such luck.

I reached the counter and showed my papers to a man in an immaculate beige uniform. He looked at me, called another man in uniform over, then waved me to the side. The new arrival looked more senior. He pointed to a plastic chair. 'Sit,' he ordered, as he strode briskly into another room with my passport.

I was surprised to hear his harsh tone of voice. In England, I'd have been off complaining to his supervisor. But this was Saudi Arabia; he was holding all the aces and I was playing my cards close to my chest.

I thought back to the many pieces of advice I'd been offered by Arab women. While we were celebrating in that

Lebanese restaurant after I received my visa, a fellow diner heard me talking. 'Remember that you are going to enter another world, where women are treated like a lower class,' she warned. 'At times you will feel you are being treated like a dog, but it is the way of the country. There's no point in fighting back, if you want to see your children.'

Recalling her words of wisdom, I sat down quietly. My scarf kept falling off and I hoped that wouldn't count against me. It was made from a slippery material and, try as I might, it kept sliding around my head. I hadn't yet mastered that particular skill. Other men in uniform walked past and looked at me, wondering what was going on.

After about ten minutes, two men appeared with my passport. One of them asked the name of my maharam. They also wanted to know who was picking me up. I gave the name of my lawyer, Abdullah, and they walked into an office. Another ten minutes later, they were back, wearing grim expressions.

'There's no one of that name outside,' one of the men said coldly, looking down at me as I sat perched on the plastic chair. He looked and sounded very official.

'Could I borrow your phone to call him?' I pleaded, knowing I was sounding desperate. I tried to sound calm but failed miserably.

The officials discussed my case for a minute, then one of them came over. 'You can't use our phone. Give me all your bags and go to the arrivals hall and find your maharam.'

This was developing into an ordeal and I'd only just landed. 'God only knows what lies ahead,' I muttered. I was panicking more and more. I'd never met Abdullah and had no idea what he looked like.

I reluctantly handed over my bags, including my handbag with all my money and papers, and wandered into the arrivals area. I was tailed by one of the Immigration men.

I was sure that they could see I was shaking. I guessed that if I didn't meet their requirements I'd be on the next plane back to Heathrow. By this time, most of the other passengers had left. No one seemed to be looking for me. I was peering around, trying to see Abdullah, hoping he was carrying a sign with my name; I was also praying that my children might be waiting too. The men all looked the same in their white robes and red headscarves. I couldn't see my children.

I must have looked dejected and downcast as I trudged back into Immigration.

'Sit,' said one of the men, and I hoped they weren't enjoying this. I was hating every second and started to cry.

Several men in uniform took it in turn to look at my passport, talking loudly in Arabic and discussing what to do with me. I asked again if I could use a phone to call Abdullah. They just waved me back to my chair without listening or answering.

After what seemed an eternity, a tall, handsome man in a traditional-looking long, white garment came storming in. He started to talk to the Immigration officials and they pointed at me. It turned out to be Abdullah's brother, Mussa. Whatever he said to them provided a quick fix. Within five minutes, he had my passport and my bags back in my possession and we were on our way out of the building.

As Mussa led me to his car, he apologised for being late. I glanced back at the arrivals hall, wishing so much that the children could have greeted me there. At the same time,

I felt stupid, thinking T would have done that for me and the children.

The heat outside was unbearable. I wished I could take off my black clothes, but I knew they were vital to my cause. The air conditioning in Mussa's car provided a welcome relief from the furnace outside.

I looked around as we approached a highway leading from the airport. I was struck by the sheer scale of everything; one of the terminals had a roof consisting of white cones, with metal poles reaching skywards. Mussa said I was looking at the Hajj Terminal, used by millions of pilgrims every year on their way to Mecca. I asked if I could borrow his mobile, and for the first time that day someone allowed me to use a phone. I scoured my address book for Uncle Adnan's number.

'Hello, Adnan, I'm here in Jeddah,' I said as soon as the phone was picked up. 'As you know, I'm here to see my children. I'm sure that you and the children all know I'm here. Can I speak to my children?'

Adnan sounded annoyed. 'Actually, this isn't really my problem. You should take this up with T. I don't know why you've bothered to call me.'

'You know damn well that T is impossible to deal with,' I countered. 'When the children were abducted, they were taken to your house, so you're in this with him. I've come to Saudi Arabia to see my children and I *will* see them.'

I don't know where all this determination and assertive talk came from, as I'd just been through a nightmare at the airport and still felt shaky. I knew, though, that this call was vital and I had to put my case exactly and perfectly.

Adnan started to raise his voice. He said the whole thing

Proudly holding my Tesco Mum of the Year award.

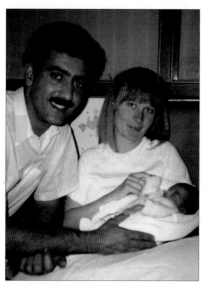

Above left: A terrible two-year-old with the face of an angel!

Above right: Wedded bliss? It didn't quite turn out that way …

Below left: New arrival – holding one of the twins shortly after he was born. As the picture shows, I was totally exhausted.

Below right: Alex shortly after his birth, dressed in keeping with tradition for his Muslim naming ceremony.

Above: Happy families. On holiday in Denmark, shortly after Adam's birth. *Back row from left to right*: my dad, Edmund, me, Adam, my sister, Ingrid, and my mum, Grethe. *Front row from left to right*: Alex, Zak and Max.

Below left: Brotherly love. My boys, all dressed up for a Balinese ceremony.

Below right: From Bali with love. I never stopped writing to my boys in the time we were apart.

Inset: My faithful maid, Bude, who was at my side until I left Bali.

Above: Absent mum. T sent me this photograph from Saudi shortly after he abducted the boys.

Below: The boys sent me so many letters and poems while we were separated. Here are just two of them.

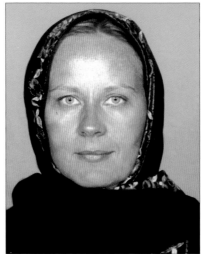

Above left: My little Adam being dropped at school in his traditional Saudi robe.

Above right: At all times while living in Saudi Arabia, I had to comply with the strict Muslim dress code.

Below: Reunited at last. The first of my precious meetings with my boys in the horrendous Saudi flat. Max took this picture of me and his three brothers.

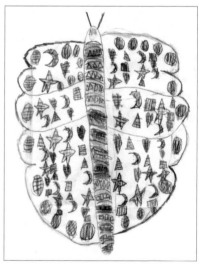

Above left: Home from home. The entrance to my compound in Jeddah, where I lived for fourteen months.

Above right: Woman in black. When this picture was taken, I had just returned from an exhausting court hearing in Saudi. Strictly speaking, I shouldn't be revealing any flesh.

Below left: Big day out. The boys and I made the most of our time together after the Saudi court granted me limited access.

Below right: This is the beautiful butterfly drawn by Adam during a dispute over access.

Above left: Zak's back! Our first summer holiday after we were reunited. I took the boys to see their family in Denmark.

Above right: A proud mum enjoying the sea air in Devon, with the boys she feared she'd never see again.

Below left: Back to school. Adam ready for his first day back in the classroom in Devon.

Below right: Pay day! Max collects his first wages for his paper round.

Party time! Celebrating my Tesco award at the Hilton in London.

Above: With my friend Tracey Howard, Professor Steve Thomas and his sister, Professor Caroline Thomas.

Below left: A star-studded cast. With former *EastEnders* actresses Pooja Shah and Jemma Walker.

Below right: The award was presented to me by Denise Carter, the director of Reunite, here on my right. Also pictured is TV presenter Matthew Wright.

was my fault; I hadn't taken care of my children properly; I'd been running around with other men; and T had heard that I'd been planning to take the children to Denmark. He was quoting T word for word, so I knew the source of his information.

I moved the conversation back to my children and asked again when I could see them. Adnan said they weren't at his house, but they would be there later in the afternoon. He started to sound more reasonable.

Perhaps that was because he'd unleashed his venom at me. Or maybe he could tell that I wasn't going to go away and he had to deal with me. I reckon it was a combination of both. I said that I'd be phoning later and we ended the conversation on reasonable terms.

Mussa drove for 45 minutes through Jeddah, towards Abdullah's house. All the buildings along the route looked spectacular, with enormous gates. I couldn't see anyone anywhere, because it was too hot for people to move around outside.

Eventually, we arrived at Abdullah's place. I noticed a sign outside giving his name and company details. I couldn't believe I had arrived at last. Here, perhaps was my chance to be reunited with my children.

Waiting at the door was a smiling English lady in her fifties. It was Abdullah's English wife, Kathy. She asked me to take off my abaya and scarf, and I was pleased to see the back of those for a while. I hung them up behind the front door, where a range of black garments cast a solemn shadow over the hallway.

As I sat there with a cold drink, Kathy could see I was in an emotional state.

'Maybe you should go to the bathroom to freshen up a bit,' she suggested in a gentle and caring voice. 'Abdullah will be here in a minute and we'll have something to eat and talk about things.'

I headed off for the bathroom and locked the door. I knew I looked awful. I had a wash and wiped away the tears that kept appearing. Glancing in the mirror, I could see that I did look awful and I was shaking. Five minutes of deep breathing helped me to pull myself together. I had to make a good impression on Abdullah.

As I emerged, feeling fresher and a little better, I could see a man in a white robe talking to Mussa in the hallway. I assumed it was Abdullah, and it was indeed the man himself.

He greeted me in the same friendly manner as Kathy, and I liked him at once. I could see that another guest had arrived. My first impression was of a beautiful, glamorous lady. She turned out to be another client of Abdullah, called Tina. She was a year younger than me and, by coincidence, also Scandinavian. Her Saudi husband had made off with her children three years earlier. We got on well from the start, exchanging our stories. Abdullah had arranged for me to stay with Tina while I was staying in Saudi Arabia.

Kathy announced that lunch was ready and I could see that the dining room was adorned with a splendid feast. I realised that I was starving, as I'd been too nervous to eat anything substantial for two days or more. After gorging on vegetable and salad dishes, I felt a whole lot better. Everyone was trying to make me feel relaxed and at home.

After lunch, Abdullah called us all into a little television room. We started talking about what was going to happen and how he could possibly help me to see the children.

The pitfalls, he explained, were many and varied. He said that there was no point in me talking to anyone, as I would get nowhere.

He asked me for Adnan's number, picked up the phone and started speaking in Arabic. He talked for what seemed a long time, at first quietly, but then his voice became loud and angry. I hoped he hadn't come up against the brick wall I'd faced earlier.

Abdullah put down the receiver and said he'd been talking to T and Adnan, and neither was sounding too co-operative. Nevertheless, they'd agreed that I could call the children at T's house at six o'clock that evening.

Around five, as the sun set on my first day in Saudi, we all travelled to Tina's house in Abdullah's car. It was a large Mercedes with white leather seats, very much in the Saudi style.

Tina lived in an attractive compound. After a few minutes getting past the security guards, I could see 30 or so small houses situated around a large swimming pool and picturesque gardens.

I was shown to my room, which had shelves full of children's toys. On the walls were children's posters. On top of a wardrobe, I saw piles of wrapped presents. I couldn't see any children around, then I remembered that Tina was in the same situation as me.

I had my eye on the watch, waiting for six o'clock to arrive. I paced around. Quarter to six ... ten to six ... five to six ... two minutes to six ... I called the number at six on the dot.

Max answered after the first ring. As I write this, I can't believe I hadn't seen him for nearly a year and a half.

147

'Hi, baby, I'm here in Saudi. I'm here. I'm in Jeddah.'

'Mummy, Mummy, Mummy. I know, I know. Uncle Adnan says we can see you tomorrow. Did you bring us any presents?'

'Of course, darling, I've got you lots of presents. You'll just have to wait and see what they are.'

I could hear the other three boys in the background, fighting to get to the phone. At the same time, I could hear T and his brother talking very loudly. I talked to Alex, Zak and Adam in turn. They sounded so happy to hear my voice that I cried again. I seemed to be crying all the time.

Max came back on the line and said Uncle Adnan wanted to talk to Abdullah. After several minutes of intense discussion on the phone, Abdullah said Adnan would pick me up at nine o'clock the next morning and take me to see the children.

It was so exciting getting presents ready for the boys. Tina and I went to the shopping mall around the corner from her compound. I bought lots of snacks, sweets and drinks that I knew the boys liked.

I was ready in good time early the next morning, and waited by the gate of the compound with my bags of goodies. Adnan arrived at exactly nine o'clock in a large, shiny American car. After a short but civilised greeting, I climbed into the front seat next to him. Normally, he explained, I'd have to travel in the back under Saudi law, but because it was Friday – a religious day – there weren't many people around and he'd take a chance. We'd both moved on from that row on the phone.

I'd expected to meet the children at Adnan's house. My heart sank when he said we were going to a flat belonging to his wife's mother. The children, he said, would be waiting for me there.

The drive across Jeddah took about 25 minutes. It was stiflingly hot, as usual, and I could see why air conditioning played an essential role in everyday life. Adnan explained the layout of the city and we chatted about general stuff, leaving the kids out of the conversation.

We arrived outside a block of flats and parked under the building. Then we both squeezed into a small lift outside the flats to reach the third floor. I had so many bags of presents that they were starting to evade my grasp. I gave up on my headscarf when it fell off for the third time, reckoning I'd have to accept my punishment if apprehended.

The lift clunked to a halt on the third floor and I could see six or seven doors. One of them began to open slowly. I caught sight of Zak peering out. My heart speed doubled. Oh, my God. Behind those doors were my four children. I let out a shriek and I yelled. I shouted out my son's name. Zak was the last boy I'd kissed goodnight, 16 months earlier. Yes, I hadn't seen my boys for *16 months*. My God, I was seeing them again now.

I dropped all my bags on the spot and ran towards Zak. I reached out and hugged him, like I'd never hugged him before. Sixteen months of no hugs at all went into that one embrace. I was overcome by emotion and tears flowed in little rivers down my cheeks.

The twins appeared from behind him. I bent down and hugged them too. Next my youngest son, Adam, appeared with a big smile on his face, and we hugged and hugged. The first thing I noticed about Adam was his big new front teeth and how tall he was.

'Mum, you look the same as when we were in Bali,' Alex said.

'Mum, yes, you do look the same,' Max chipped in, and I was glad to hear it.

'You both look the same, just a lot more grown up,' I told them.

'I missed you lots, Mum,' Zak said during his umpteenth hug. 'Why did you take so long to come?'

'What's in all those bags, Mum?' Adam wanted to know.

I remembered I'd dropped them, but Adnan did the honours and brought the gifts into the flat.

I took a quick look round and it was obvious that no one lived in the flat. We went into a room with a sofa, a table and two armchairs. A Filipino maid came in and took my abaya. Adnan told me I had two hours with the boys and handed me a piece of paper. He was in an awkward position, acting as a go-between.

Written on the scruffy paper in T's handwriting were the times I could see my boys: Mondays, Wednesdays and Saturdays from ten in the morning until midday. And that was it. I had to be thankful for this smallest of mercies and, despite our differences, I knew I was indebted to Adnan.

The boys were pulling me in all directions, all talking at the same time and still asking what was in the bags. First, I produced their snacks and drinks, and those all disappeared rapidly. Next, they opened the parcels containing new clothes and toys. I noticed that they were wearing old-fashioned worn-out trainers, so I measured their feet and promised to buy them new ones.

I could see that the maid was sitting just outside the room

next to a large mirror and that the mirror was directly opposite another room. I was being watched.

I hugged the boys in turn, again and again, and tried to divide my time equally between them, talking and playing. It was so lovely to be with them once more. It felt as if we'd never been apart. When I asked them about their stepmum, they told me that T and his wife were no longer together. They argued a lot and she'd moved back to her family. The children also told me that the Saudi wife was having a baby. Adam was upset that she'd left, but the older boys weren't bothered.

I took out the ITV video camera to record our reunion. I planned to send the pictures back to the TV company, and also to my friends and family in Denmark. Within seconds of starting to film, Adnan came storming into the room. He told me in no uncertain terms that I wasn't allowed to do any filming.

I reckoned that the maid had been told to signal if I began filming, or perhaps if I tried to take the children out of the third-floor window! Adnan was sitting in another room, watching the maid via the mirror.

The two hours passed far too quickly, and very soon the maid brought my abaya. She said it was time to leave and that the driver was waiting downstairs to take me home. Adnan had several cars, and several children. He shared out the motoring with this driver. The boys all went quiet and looked sad. I tried to cheer them up, saying we'd see each other in a few days' time.

Adam just hung on to me and wouldn't let me go, but I had to put him down and it felt as if a knife had been driven through my heart. Before leaving, I hugged and kissed all the boys. The maid escorted me downstairs, where a car was waiting for me, and she told me to sit in the back.

As we pulled away, I looked out of the rear window and glimpsed T getting out of a car parked behind us. I could see him glaring and walking towards the flats. Suddenly, I felt anger welling up inside me. I wanted to shout, 'Stop the car!', but I remembered what someone from the Saudi Embassy had said about how I must behave, so I kept quiet. Instead, I turned my thoughts to the boys and made plans for our next meeting, two days later.

On the plus side, I was able to call them at their home any time, and I guessed Adnan was responsible for that. They'd broken up from school and now had a long summer holiday in front of them. They couldn't understand why they weren't allowed to spend more time with me. Why did they have to go to that awful flat to see me?

The boys knew I wanted to take them shopping and spend some quality time together. They nagged T to let them spend more hours with me. He told them they could only see me in the flat and he was too busy to take them for extra visits.

By now, I was becoming really frustrated. When I talked to the children on the phone, they always sounded bored. They didn't go outside and just played with their PlayStation and computer games, or watched television all day. My lawyer, Abdullah, said I was lucky to see them at all and I should count my blessings. I had absolutely no rights in Saudi Arabia. I got the point.

I had to find things to do when I wasn't seeing the children. Tina was a fabulous companion. We spoke Scandinavian together and she took me to see the grand shopping malls. I bought new clothes, shoes and toys for the boys. At night, we had long, involved chats about our respective situations; she missed her kids just as much as I missed mine. We also visited Abdullah's house for sumptuous dinners. I met many of Tina's friends and we sat outside at her compound soaking up the cool night air.

While I was there, the twins' twelfth birthday came along. I phoned Adnan, making a plea to see them on their special day. I tried to remain calm and speak in a civilised manner. Tina was listening in and I could hear her saying that I was being too polite. She was making gestures to me, suggesting that I should press my case more forcibly.

When Tina shouted that the children had been stolen and God would punish T, Adnan heard what she was saying in the background and he started to shout too, with me in the middle of all this commotion. He yelled in my ear that the stupid woman in the background should not interfere and she didn't have a clue about Islam. T was in charge of the boys, he said, and could do whatever he liked. Then he slammed the phone down.

So I didn't see the twins on their birthday, but two days later instead. For our get-together, I bought cakes, hats, decorations and lots of presents. The driver picked me up from Tina's compound. This time it appeared that only a maid and the boys were in the flat. However, I learned later that T was also in one of the back rooms. I felt very uneasy during that visit, especially as I saw the maid locking the front door and disappearing with the keys into a room at the back of the flat.

We enjoyed two beautiful hours. Again, the boys loved their presents, they enjoyed our time together and we had our own little party. We sat with our hats on, played party games and all laughed. All too soon, it was time to leave again.

I put up with the visiting hours during that three-and-a-half-week visit to Saudi Arabia; I had no choice. During my free time, though, I found out about how to get a job. Could I get a job? I had to find one, because it was a way of ensuring that I could return to the country. Abdullah told me that international schools were always looking for teachers. It so happened that one of his former clients was a school headmistress called Mrs Fatin. She ran an Arabic English International School. That meant they did teach Arabic, but English was also on the curriculum, so I knew I could fit in.

I made an appointment to see Mrs Fatin, who hired me straight away and started the proceedings for my working visa. I spent two mornings at the school, met other teachers and learned as much as I could about the system.

I couldn't tell the boys about the job; I couldn't risk T finding out, so I stayed quiet. That was hard, because I was so excited and keen to tell them I was coming back. One misplaced word could have put my entire plans in jeopardy.

The last meeting with my children was on the day I was due to fly home. I gave them an envelope each with pocket money and bought them more clothes and toys. I'd managed to take some still pictures and compiled a small album for them.

I couldn't even comfort my sons by saying I was coming back soon. They all clung on to me and wouldn't let go. I managed to hold back my tears until I reached the lift outside that horrendous flat. I had just endured the hardest of all goodbyes.

Now it was time to learn everything – and I mean everything – about Saudi Arabia.

12

A FLAVOUR OF SAUDI

S audi Arabia is a total culture shock to Westerners.
When I started out on my quest to rescue my children
from the desert, I really didn't have a clue about what I was
up against. I knew very little about the written and
unwritten rules and how women are expected to behave.

By 'behave', I mean so that they can be seen as
respectable. An example might be that when a female gets
into a taxi she must sit as far away from the driver as
possible. So, if she clambers in directly behind him, that's
not acceptable. The lady has to seek out the farthest corner
of the cab and perch herself there.

Women can only mix freely with certain male relatives.
These are grandfathers, fathers, brothers from the same
father, maternal and paternal uncles and sons. You don't
have to cover yourself up when you're with these people.
When a woman passes a man in the street, shopping
centre, supermarket or anywhere, she must look down.

No eye contact with a man is permitted – unless he's a family member.

The worth of a female in Saudi Arabia is very low. A woman can't be responsible for herself at any age. Women get only half of a man's share of inheritance. Their testimony in court isn't worth nearly as much as that given by a man. A husband, father or uncle can decide whether a woman attends university, works or travels.

When it comes to custody rights, mothers have none. Islamic law rules in this area. The main concern of Saudi courts is to make sure that a boy or girl is raised in accordance with the Islamic faith. Custody isn't normally granted to a Saudi woman; if you're not a Saudi, forget it!

When a marriage breaks down, a mother can have custody of the children until a boy is nine and a girl is seven. They believe that, after this age, the mother's care isn't needed any more and the primary care is transferred to the father. If the mother remarries before that time, she loses the children, especially in the case of girls. That is because a young girl isn't allowed to live in the same house as a male who isn't a relative.

Sharia law dictates that, in the case of the death or imprisonment of a father, custody of the children goes to the closest male relative. This can happen even if the Saudi father has made clear that the children's mother should have full custody.

I was fortunate to be allowed into Saudi Arabia. When I returned home, I looked at many websites and they said it was virtually impossible to get in. As far as I can see, T could have made more of a fuss about my presence in the country. An ex-husband often objects to a visit by the mother of his children, on grounds of emotional disruption for the children. The husband's second wife can become jealous and that's a common reason for banning visits.

Was I lucky, or what! I read on a family-law website that only one American wife had successfully made no-objection visits over a period of five years. She was successful because she spoke Arabic and managed to maintain steady relations with her ex-husband. She had to accept, though, that her child would spend at least his first 18 years in Saudi Arabia.

In divorce cases, men can finalise the marriage with a simple oath; women must make their cases before the judiciary.

I mentioned earlier that there's a problem with eye contact. Basically, avoid it with any member of the opposite sex. Also, the opposite sexes should never show any affection in public, and this even applies to married couples.

The standard Muslim greeting is 'As-salam alaykum', or 'Peace be upon you'. The reply has a subtle difference: 'Wa alaykum as-salam', 'And upon you, peace'. There is a whole series of other ritual greetings and replies.

One of the first things I was told when I arrived in the country as a teacher was not to expose the soles of my shoes, even accidentally. I always remembered this when I sat down and crossed my legs. I also had to be careful with phrases referring to footwear, such as 'put yourself in my shoes'.

I had a list I used to refer to. For example, in class I had to be careful about using an upright finger to beckon someone over, as that can be interpreted as insulting. It's best to turn the hand so that the palm is facing downwards, then move all the fingers towards your body.

Men in Saudi often greet one another with kisses. However, the males usually just shake hands with foreign men unless they're close friends. The handshake can be an ordeal, as Saudi men really grip and press hard. It would be insensitive to withdraw your hand at this stage, so, if you want to remain friends, just endure the pain.

Men and women don't shake hands. A Western man, meeting a Saudi man in the street accompanied by his wife, won't even be introduced to the woman. Many Saudi men, when they meet a Western couple, won't acknowledge the presence of the wife.

Serious discussions are often pre-empted by small talk, either business or pleasure. Saudis regard a person who wants to get to the point straight away as being rude or impatient. I learned to ask how a person was keeping; then I enquired about the health of the other family members. It's impolite for a man to ask about the welfare of a wife or another female member of the family.

Saudis show tremendous respect for their elders. Age takes precedence over status, and the eldest person is always greeted first. At a function, an elderly guest is given the most prominent seating position and receives food and drink before anyone else. There is an exception. When a high-ranking member of the Royal Family is present, they can expect preferential treatment, but even a royal visitor usually defers to age.

The Saudis can be very hospitable. It's a great honour to be invited to a Saudi home. It's normal to politely refuse once or twice before accepting a spontaneous invitation. If the invitation is written, it's best to reply in Arabic if possible.

Men and women eat separately, as I mentioned earlier when discussing our local mosque in England. Many Saudi families, especially in the cities, now eat at a table and from my experience most now use cutlery. When I ventured out into the desert, I found that families ate on the floor and used their hands.

It's crucial to remember that only the right hand should be used for eating. A spoon may be offered to foreigners, but it's more courteous to eat with the fingers. It's customary to thank God after the meal and to wash the hands and mouth. The right hand is used for the meal, as the left hand is reserved for washing after using the loo, because in Saudi Arabia – as in most other Arab countries – toilet paper isn't used. There's always plenty of water available next to the toilet.

Later in the book, I refer to men wearing thobes. These are bright white, full-length and long-sleeved. I thought the men looked handsome in them. Under the thobes, they wear long pantaloons called sirwaal. Many men now wear European-style shoes but leather sandals, or na'al, are still common and have colourful patterns.

The south-west of the country is steeped in tradition and a lot of men – particularly the older ones – still wear a djambiya. This is a curved dagger in a decorated sheath and is worn at official or ceremonial occasions.

The men's white cotton headdress is a ghutra and the red-and-white checked one is a sham'agh, but nowadays the first term is used loosely for both. Most men wear their headdress most of the time, and it's seen as rude if you ask them to remove it.

Saudi Arabia is basically a collection of large cities in the desert. There's not much colour, there's little to do and the laws are tough. There's no tourism, no green hills and everything is man-made. You get the impression that your surroundings aren't natural, and you live in an air-conditioned environment day and night.

Most of the year it's hot, and I mean roasting. It's not the most pleasant experience, walking around in a compulsory black abaya when it's over 40 degrees centigrade. You can't leave home without it. A matching headscarf to cover your hair must be worn outside the home at all times. During my court hearings in Saudi, I reckon I was frying in 50 degrees and covered from head to toe (black socks and black gloves included).

The abaya can be made from silk, cotton or synthetic material. They're all black, of course, but nowadays you can buy designer garments, and they can be embroidered with silver and gold thread. The cities are full of shops selling abayas and matching scarves with traditional and modern designs.

In a remote village, you will see a girl wearing a basic black abaya which could be made for virtually nothing; a princess in a royal palace will wear a silk garment decorated with precious stones and embroidered with gold and silver thread.

A plain gauze veil is used to cover a woman's face. In some areas, leather masks are worn; in others, ladies wear a mask known as a burqa that has only an opening for the eyes. Saudi women, especially the Bedouins, love wearing jewellery. It indicates status and, in times of need, is converted into cash.

Earlier, I mentioned learning about the evil eye when T's brother came to Exeter with his new wife. So I went to Saudi prepared, but I still made a mistake in a supermarket – although I didn't see it as a mistake at the time. I was waiting at a checkout in Jeddah with my friend Tina, when I saw a woman carrying a gorgeous baby. She was such a beautiful child, with a big mop of thick, curly, black hair. With all the trauma going on in my life and missing the kids desperately, I gazed at the lovely child. I was thinking about my absent babies too, and I just stood there and enjoyed the experience for a minute. I said to Tina, 'Look at the lovely baby's hair!'

The mother saw I was looking at the baby, and in a flash her expression changed. If looks could kill, I would have died on the spot. Tina reacted quickly, to save me from further embarrassment. She pushed me to the side and told me the mother thought I'd given her child the evil eye. If anything were to happen to the baby's hair in the future, she would blame it on me. OK, I'm a dumb blonde. I never thought of that one. Tina pointed out that the incident showed why Muslims rarely exchange compliments. Look at what can happen!

The biggest issue, I found, was making sure that hair, legs, arms and the body were covered correctly. You can't leave your house without the all-important abaya, and your hair must be hidden.

You're always fiddling with your headscarf, making sure your hair doesn't fall down. I had to ensure that my flowing golden strands didn't make an unwelcome appearance in the open air.

When I first arrived in Saudi, I was in awe of the place. Wealth on such a grand scale is difficult to comprehend to begin with. I reckon that some of the richer families there must have more money than some countries in the region. The economy took off after oil was discovered in 1938, and clearly the Saudis haven't looked back.

A powerful expression of that wealth is the fabulous Hajj

Terminal at the airport in Jeddah. Completed in the early 1980s, it's a quarter bigger than the Pentagon. The award-winning design of the roof is based on Bedouin tents and serves to remind the two million pilgrims who pass through the terminal each year of their desert-dwelling ancestors. The enormous building is made up of 21 tent units, each 150 feet square, hanging from suspension cables. The terminal provides astonishing facilities for the pilgrims, catering for their every need. It's a marvel of modern architecture.

The Kingdom of Saudi Arabia is the largest country on the Arabian Peninsula. It borders Jordan, Iraq, Kuwait, Qatar, Bahrain, the United Arab Emirates, Oman and Yemen. The Persian Gulf lies to the north-east and the Red Sea to the west. The country is mostly semi-desert and desert with oases. Almost half of the land mass is uninhabitable desert. In most regions, annual rainfall is no more than four inches and there is extreme heat and aridity. It's one of the few places in the world where summer temperatures above 50 degrees are common. Surprisingly, amid all this heat, the higher mountains do have the occasional coating of snow.

Few people from the West have had the opportunity to experience all this, however, because of the country's restrictions on tourism. When I first tried to go there, the only visas available covered pilgrimages, employment and visiting. I couldn't get a visiting visa, because, as I said earlier, I had no Muslim family member or maharam to sponsor me.

You can see why I was confused to read, while I was writing this book, that Saudi was beginning to open its doors to tourists. Somehow I can't see discos, bars, nightclubs or casinos operating in such a restricted society.

Yet the newspapers and websites definitely envisaged non-Muslim visitors seeking out Saudi's hidden treasures.

At the time of writing, there's what you could call limited access. My research in July 2006 uncovered an article, possibly compiled without enough checks, which announced that 'Saudi Arabia seems an unlikely destination for fun in the sun'. It went on to say that a Saudi prince was busily trying to sell his country as a vacation spot 'provided that visitors don't expect alcohol, women come robed and everyone refrains from eating in public from dawn to dusk during the holy month of Ramadan'.

Here are the positive bits. Although the holiest of sites such as Mecca and Media are off-limits to non-Muslims, there are hundreds of cultural and archaeological sites, including an ancient rose-coloured city, carved in sandstone, and dating back to several hundred years BC.

There are spectacular opportunities for scuba diving. Conditions are perfect along 1,000 miles of the Red Sea coast and 500 miles of the Persian Gulf. I mentioned earlier that the coral reefs around Bali were threatened by overfishing and pollution; off Saudi Arabia, they're virtually untouched. Scuba diving in such idyllic conditions appeals to me, but would I have to wear a black robe? My black socks could double up as flippers maybe, but I can't see how I'd get round the rules.

Yes, that does sound cynical, but remember I've lived there and, despite the publicity surround the issuing of tourism-type visas, I decided to put all this to the test. I'd read several stories about the country opening up to tourists, so I thought I'd carry out some additional research. I picked up the phone and called the visa section at the Saudi Embassy in London.

'I'd like to enquire about tourist visas,' I told a polite Arabic-sounding gentleman. 'I'd love to visit Saudi Arabia to see all the sights.'

Well, I don't think a Danish blonde would have any chance of being let loose at any tourist sites there – with or without a male sponsor – but I reckon he had a stock answer.

'Tourist visas are not being issued yet,' he told me. 'Call back in a few months.' He was pleasant and matter-of-fact, but I didn't get any further. He sounded as if he had to say the same thing several times a day. By the time you read this, things may have changed, but that was the position in mid-2006.

Saudi Arabia is known as 'the land of the two holy mosques', referring of course to Islam's two holiest places, Mecca and Medina. Access to the two holy cities is strictly forbidden to all non-Muslims. Over a billion Muslims throughout the world face Mecca five times daily in prayer. Non-Muslims can't get a glimpse of it. An eight-lane highway leads there from Jeddah, 45 miles away, and if you're a non-believer your car is diverted away from the holy city. There are road checks all the way there. They check your identity card; if you're a Muslim it's green, while a red one is issued to Christians. It's a failsafe system.

For every Muslim, it's a major expression of faith to make the pilgrimage to the holy Ka'aba, the shrine in the centre of the grand mosque in Mecca, at least once in a lifetime. Islam's first place of worship was built here. It's believed that there is a direct path from this shrine to heaven.

Saudi Arabia doesn't allow religious freedom and forbids all forms of non-Muslim public worship, although non-

Muslims are allowed to worship in their own homes. To attempt to convert a Muslim to Christianity is a serious crime.

When a baby is born, the child is bathed immediately and then given to the mother. The father or the imam whispers the call to prayer in the child's ears. That's the first sound it hears about the Muslim faith. The father also whispers the baby's name in its ear three times. T performed this act with all four of our children.

A Muslim male is usually circumcised within the first seven days. If that's not possible for a medical reason, it is performed before puberty.

The country's laws are based on the Holy Book, the Qur'an, and Islam governs most aspects of daily life. The system is also known as Sharia. An outsider looking in might think some of the punishments are harsh. However, I found that the Saudis take great pride in their reputation of having a well-ordered society. Generally, they won't interfere with what you do if it's done quietly, privately and discreetly.

But what if you're caught breaking the country's laws? Well, Embassy staff from your country will do what they can to help foreign nationals in this position. However, they don't have any power to prevent punishment being meted out. If you're caught drinking alcohol, you face the prospect of several lashes. I enjoy a glass of wine myself and can think of occasions where I could have had one. In my situation, though, it just wasn't worth taking the risk, as I could have lost everything. Anyone caught with equipment for making alcohol doesn't get off lightly either. The most likely sentence is prison, then deportation.

Around the time I was there, a British expatriate was sentenced to eight years in prison and ordered to receive 800 lashes. He was also fined £400,000 for allegedly running an illegal drinking den. He fled to Dubai, but was extradited to Saudi Arabia to face his accusers. Reports at the time said the man wasn't allowed to have a lawyer. Later, I read that he was allowed back to Britain after serving part of his sentence. His punishment does seem harsh, but remember that everyone knows the risks.

Of course, the stories about foreign Embassy staff enjoying a drink are true. It's customary that diplomatic bags enter countries without being checked, which means that staff do have access to alcohol on special occasions. I know this happens.

Shortly after I arrived in the country, I made friends with a nurse who worked at a hospital in Jeddah. She told me that bingeing on drink and drugs had become a major issue. She described how young Saudi people were brought in unconscious and some of them died.

'You have to work as a nurse or another job on the front line to know all this is going on,' she told me over coffee after her shift. 'The problem is that people over here have no experience of alcohol. They don't see adults drinking, have no relationship with alcohol and don't know how to manage it. They get hold of a bottle of whisky and drink it all. Mix that with drugs, and it can be a lethal combination.'

'I've heard about parties where they serve alcohol,' I told her. 'I didn't realise there was a full-scale industry going on here.'

'It's all swept under the carpet,' my nurse friend pointed out. 'You'll never read about it. Wealthy kids can get hold of whatever they want, and I see the results every day. Also, remember that in the West people are used to alcohol and, in some cases, drugs. They're not used to it here, so they end up polluting their bodies with enormous one-off binges.'

'I can imagine', I said, recalling a couple of ghastly drunken sessions in my teenage years. I'd never tried hard drugs, but I got her point.

As the months went by, I discovered more and more about this underworld, which officially doesn't even exist. The main elements are drink, drugs, porn and prostitution. From the outside, you'd never believe everything that goes on. I can assure you, it does.

It's worth knowing what happens to people who commit what are regarded as really serious offences. Murderers are put to death. Shortly after I arrived, I discovered that the same fate awaits anyone who commits adultery or homosexual acts.

Drug smugglers are also executed. Even a minor trafficker who repeats the offence can lose his or her life. Expect a two-year prison sentence for possession of even the smallest quantity. From what I was told, the prisons are generally overcrowded and very hot. Exercise is an occasional privilege. Jail is intended as punishment and rehabilitation doesn't come into it.

The chosen method of execution is usually beheading, carried out in public. A thief who keeps flouting the law will have his right hand cut off. This is also a public event, carried out once a week in the town square after the Friday prayers.

Don't get into debt, because, if you can't pay what you owe, you face the wrath of the Saudi authorities. Under Sharia law, you'll be jailed, but going to prison doesn't discharge the debt; you still must find a way of paying it when you're released.

I found that, as well as avoiding personal debt, it's vital to keep a careful note of anything given to you by an employer. That covers anything which passes through your hands. If you're a company representative in Saudi, and the company owes money, you can be held personally responsible.

Keeping an eye on everyone, and making sure Sharia law is obeyed, are the Mutaween, the 'religious' or 'public order' police, whose full title is the Committee for the Propagation of Virtue and Prevention of Vice. They number around 3,500 officers, plus many volunteers, and enforce Saudi Arabia's interpretation of Sharia (which is interpreted differently by the various Islamist theocracies). Their wide-ranging and seemingly arbitrary powers cover surveillance, entry to property, detention and interrogation of suspects, summary judgment and punishment, including flogging and execution, of those found guilty under Sharia. These powers permit them to enforce dress codes, dietary laws and prayer schedules, and to arrest unrelated males and females caught mixing together.

To me their remit seemed endless. They're always on the lookout for anyone who has the slightest link with alcohol or pork. They can seize banned consumer products such as CDs, DVDs or films.

Another important function of the Mutaween is to prevent the practice of other religions. To this end, they're happy to receive tip-offs from informers and so they operate a website where people can report 'un-Islamic' activities, or alternatively there's a telephone number. Informers remain anonymous, of course.

While their main role is to police Muslims, the Mutaween take considerable interest in the behaviour of non-Muslim residents and visitors, and tend to be less tolerant towards them. The thought of someone contacting them to say I was talking to someone, or chewing gum, seems beyond belief. But that's what happens; luckily, no one must have spotted me during my off-guard moments.

Not long before I arrived, I saw on TV that the Mutaween had stopped schoolgirls escaping from a burning building in Mecca. It appeared that, because the girls weren't wearing headscarves or abayas, they were denied escape routes. Fifteen of them died and 50 were injured and, although I heard about the tragedy on the BBC, I wondered if it could really be true. Well, having lived in the country, I have no doubts whatsoever that it happened. The thought of those children suffering needlessly made me feel sick, and filled me with rage.

I saw on Fox News that the religious police had declared Barbie dolls a threat to morality. The report said that the revealing clothes of the 'Jewish' toy were offensive to Islam. The Mutaween launched a campaign against Barbie, coinciding with the start of the school year. The idea was to remind parents and children of the dolls' negative qualities. The dolls have been banned in Saudi for many years, but there's a thriving black market. If you get caught, you and the doll will be in big trouble.

Muslims follow a lunar calendar of 12 months. The months are shorter, so the year ends ten days earlier than the traditional calendar used in the West. In the ninth month of the Muslim year comes Ramadan, when no Muslim must allow anything to pass between his or her lips between sunrise and sunset. The festival continues for the entire month.

No one should eat, drink or smoke in public during the

fasting hours and there are strict penalties in Saudi, such as deportation. Muslims under the age of ten aren't expected to fast, although they may try for perhaps half a day. After the age of ten, they must join in.

During Ramadan, the entire atmosphere changes, and everyone becomes really holy. Some people's religious observance may have faltered at other times during the year. It might not always have been possible to pray five times a day, go to a mosque once a week or stick to the strict Islamic dietary rules. In extreme cases, an illegal glass of lager may have been consumed. During Ramadan, though, all laws are obeyed, almost without exception.

There's a unique festive feel to this holy month, and the food has to be seen, touched and tasted to be believed. Remember that during Ramadan you fast from sunrise to sunset. When the light fades, you're starving and can't wait to hear the call for prayers from the mosque. Traditionally, the fast will be broken with dates and buttermilk (delicious), then after prayers you eat, eat and eat. A typical meal might comprise samosas, rice, meats, salads and a variety of fruits.

The whole idea of Ramadan is to make someone feel what it's like to be poor. Well, that's not really the case nowadays. Certainly, you do find out what it's like to be really hungry, but the enormous feast afterwards makes you feel far from poor.

The lavish five-star hotels put on massive feasts after sunset, about six o'clock, when the fast is broken. I remember that in Jeddah the Hilton, Sheraton and similar establishments arranged enormous buffets. The food is Arabic, Italian, Chinese, Indian and Japanese, with delicacies from other countries too, and it's not too expensive. Tina and I often went out and broke the fast in a spectacular way.

There are two major public holidays during the year, and they are very important religious festivals. Eid lasts for two weeks and celebrates the end of Ramadan. Eid al-Adha, about two months later, lasts for about ten days.

Eid al-Adha celebrates the sacrifice made by the prophet Abraham, who faced the test of killing his own son on God's command. As it turned out, this was a test for Abraham, because when he opened his eyes he had killed a lamb, not his son. That is why, during Eid al-Adha, Muslims all over the world sacrifice a lamb, sheep, camel or cow.

Christmas isn't celebrated, although, if you have some decorations in your own home, no one is going to complain. However, expatriates who want the day off are in for a shock, as it's a working day.

Oh, and don't drink the water. The country has massive desalination plants, but I was told just to use the water for showering and bathing. Everyone drinks bottled water. There's no ground water in Saudi Arabia, and so no system of pipes. Lorries transport water from the desalination plants and deliver it to houses. They fill up huge tanks beneath each home. Septic tanks are used for sewage.

Until the 1930s, there was only one tree in Jeddah. There was no fresh water, so nothing would grow in the country. Now the skyline is dominated by a desalination plant and it helps to feed more than eight million trees. Ironically, Jeddah now has the world's highest water fountain, rising more than 800 feet. It's an incredible sight, especially after dark, when the fountain is illuminated.

One thing struck me about the food. The Saudis seem to eat

meat with everything, so it's a very high-fat diet. There's no bacon, of course, but they make rashers out of other meats.

People do eat fresh salads and gorgeous herbs, grown in the mountain areas. Vegetables aren't so tasty, though. Most of them don't grow in Saudi, but are imported. They taste of chemicals used to prolong the shelf life. All containers coming into Saudi are checked thoroughly for drugs and other illegal imports, so everything sits around the ports for ages before reaching the shops.

The strong emphasis on meat – apart from pork – meant I had to keep an eye on my figure. I'm a slim size 10 as I write this, but any longer out there and I'd have ballooned.

One thing I noticed is that no one seems to get any exercise. Women in particular don't do very much, so they tend to put on weight. No one walks anywhere. It's considered unsafe for women to walk along the street; usually a married woman has a driver who covers the school run and takes her wherever she wants to go. She's not busy in the house because maids do most of the work and, of course, she doesn't go for walks.

At one time, women could go to gyms, but all that's changed now. As I understand it, the authorities became concerned when secret pictures were taken of Princess Diana in a gym. The Mutaween used this as an excuse to close down some establishments where women could meet and enjoy exercise. I was told this by other women I met there, and they didn't go to any gyms, so those are my sources! There are plenty of gyms out there, but for men only.

The religious police don't like women gathering together, except in the home. They try their best to discourage this because, without men around, the women might get ideas and become difficult to control. It's easier to control individuals than to deal with a group.

I found that, with so little to do, there's a lot of boredom in the population. There are no nightclubs, cinemas, theatres or restaurants where single men and women can eat together. In all Saudi restaurants, there are two sections; one for families and the other for single men. Single women go in the family section, and you'll rarely see a lady on her own.

When you go shopping, you'll see a wide choice of supermarkets. They carry the full range of goods you'd find in Western shops, but obviously you won't find your favourite six-pack of beer. You'll find a lot of single men and teenagers hanging around outside the supermarkets and shopping malls, mainly to get a glimpse of females walking in and out. There's little else for them to do.

Being a Westerner, I had many more options for my spare time. These included visiting beach resorts in Jeddah, owned by big hotel chains such as Sheraton. There are artificial beaches, swimming pools, beach huts, restaurants and everything else you'd expect.

Only non-Saudis are allowed inside, because the Saudis have their own resorts. So why this division? It means that both sections of society can be catered for. In the Western section, women can sunbathe and swim without being covered up. But you can forget the poolside gin and tonic.

In the Saudi area, the beach huts are more enclosed. You can't see much inside. The women are allowed outside only if they're completely covered up, so they spend most of their time inside. The men, boys and young girls play beside the pool.

I looked through the fence that overlooked their

swimming pool and I could see only men and children having a great time. I noticed a few women sitting around, under umbrellas, completely covered up.

That's the way of the Saudi people, and I respect that, but I did find the sight disturbing. I could see that, in a few years' time, those little girls would be swapping places with the covered-up ladies and having to watch all the fun instead of taking part.

My friend Tina and I used to spend weekends at these resorts. We felt it was the only place we could let our hair down and relax. Entering the resort felt like going into another country; it bore no resemblance to the rest of Saudi Arabia.

During one of those weekends, we were joined by my lawyer, Abdullah, and his wife. Abdullah is a Saudi, but he was able to get in because Kathy is English.

During our afternoon of relaxing by the pool, Kathy received a call on her mobile from her friend Isabella. She was married to Osama Bin Laden's brother. Yes, Osama Bin Laden's brother. The Bin Laden family is massive, powerful and wealthy beyond anything that most people could ever imagine. I could see that Kathy was looking excited as she talked to Isabella. I couldn't wait for her to get off the phone and tell me what was going on.

'That was the wife of Osama Bin Laden's brother,' she said. 'We've been invited out to their horse ranch for dinner.'

Horse ranch? A horse ranch in the desert? With the Bin Ladens? I sort of hoped that Osama himself wouldn't drop by. We left the resort and Abdullah pointed his rather large Mercedes inland, towards the desert.

With those Bin Laden thoughts still in my head, the monstrous Merc followed the desert track. We drove further and further away from built-up areas. I remember seeing nothing at all apart from a few Bedouins with their camels, plus sand, sand and more sand.

I thought at first it was a mirage, shimmering under the bluest sky I'd ever seen. It was no mirage. I was looking at the walls of this horse ranch. The walls were so high, they were all that an outsider could see.

Abdullah stopped at the huge gates and chatted to a security guard. The gates opened and we went through into a parking area. Then we walked to the other end of the compound, where we saw an entrance to a large building. The horses were kept there; opposite was an exercise area for the animals.

We were greeted by Bin Laden's wife, a charming Brazilian lady in her fifties. Isabella was totally down-to-earth, had glistening black hair and wore a huge smile. I took to her immediately.

She showed us around the stables. It really was a five-star hotel for horses; they wanted for nothing. I don't know much about horses, but I could tell these were the creme de la creme. They were beautifully presented, dined on the finest imported food and enjoyed luxurious surroundings, cooled by air conditioning and attended by uniformed staff.

A black stallion caught my eye. I was mesmerised as I caught sight of this stunning creature; it was as if someone had drawn a picture of a perfect horse. It was tall, slender, athletic and gleaming all at once. I asked about the stallion and was told it had fathered hundreds of top thoroughbreds. Its sperm sold for $10,000 a shot. That sounded a lot to me, until I heard about the prize money these quality breeds could win.

I emerged from the stables still feeling stunned. I could see tables laid out in a courtyard, with men sitting around and wearing traditional Saudi costumes. Many were using their laptops, and for all I knew they could have been betting on the 3.30 at Aintree!

A tall imposing figure dressed in a white thobe caught my eye. I knew at once it was Isabella's husband. He certainly looked very much like Osama Bin Laden. He greeted us enthusiastically. You can imagine that, as I looked at this man, I kept thinking of the pictures of Osama Bin Laden. I couldn't help it; it felt like a natural reaction. He came across as a nice person and couldn't do enough to please his guests.

The food arrived, which took my mind off my unexpected host for the day. By now, the party had swollen to about 40 people, and a team of caterers scurried around making sure everyone received the best of attention. We feasted on all types of Arab meat dishes with salad, bread, hummus and a host of delicacies. It was a surreal experience. Here I was, as evening fell and the sun set over the desert landscape, enjoying a banquet with the Bin Ladens. Just for the record, Osama didn't make an appearance.

On the way back, we encountered more Bedouins. Abdullah described their fascinating history for me. He said they were nomadic people who inhabited the deserts of the Middle East and North Africa. In ancient times, their territory included only the deserts of Egypt and Syria, but gradually they spread as far as Mesopotamia. As far back as the 7th century, the Muslim conquest of North Africa opened up large areas to the Bedouins. Wherever they inhabit, these people cover a great deal of territory but comprise only a fraction of the population.

As I looked out of the car at these weather-beaten people with their camels, I could see the centuries etched in their faces. I read on the internet that they weren't welcome in some countries. Apparently, their flocks had destroyed natural ground cover in many countries by overgrazing. Pastureland had turned into semi-desert in some areas and many countries were trying to curtail the Bedouins' movements.

Many of the tribes have maintained their nomadic way of life. They exist mainly on meat, milk and dairy products. Nowadays, though, many Bedouins can be found working in the oil industry. Fewer than 10 per cent of them enjoy a full nomadic lifestyle, but even the oil-industry workers return to the desert whenever they can.

The one pastime most Saudis enjoy is satellite television. It has taken off in a big way and everyone seems to be addicted. Officially, it's banned, but most households have a satellite system.

There are magnificent shopping malls with household names such as Habitat, Next and BHS. They're fitted out with marble and chandeliers and the shops carry the latest designer goods. There are no fitting rooms because the Mutaween don't allow women to undress in shops. So, if you buy a dress you just have to guess the size and take it home. If the garment doesn't fit, you exchange it.

The call to prayer comes five times a day, and all businesses, schools, government offices and shops have to close. The department stores are emptied and the security grilles descend. I found it all too much. My compound was next to a mosque, so you can imagine I didn't get much peace. During prayers, television is interrupted. The screen goes blank, apart from a still shot of Mecca and a message saying that it's time for prayers.

I went to the shops a lot, because there isn't much else to do, and I found that clothes and household goods are really cheap. CDs are also much cheaper than in Britain, because there's no tax on them, or anything else for that matter. And there are plenty of counterfeit goods, such as computer games and DVDs, available at the open-air markets. It's also worth mentioning that you don't see any female shop assistants. Companies don't employ them, in case they get chatted up by bored males. Incidentally, boredom is widespread in Saudi and I believe it prompts religious extremism in some individuals.

The traditional way of meeting is matching up boy and girl through arranged marriages. The mothers of the future husband and wife often meet at family weddings and make the arrangements there. They sit and talk together and the prospective bride is often dressed beautifully to impress the boy's mother. The future groom won't see his potential wife at that particular matchmaking event because, as in all aspects of Saudi life, the sexes are separated.

It's up to the two mums to arrange for a meeting between their respective son and daughter. It takes place in one of the two family homes, and the girl is still covered up, although the future lovers can talk to each other. If all goes well, more meetings are arranged and an engagement is announced. He might see her face, depending on how religious the families are, but he won't catch a glimpse of her hair. After that, hopefully, true love follows its normal course and they get married and live happily ever after.

Of course, not everyone wants an arranged marriage.

People from all walks of life do occasionally fancy someone. So how do men and women meet, unofficially, without families getting involved? Well, there are shopping malls and banks just for women. A lady who is attracted to a male heads off for her local shopping mall. She gets her driver to drop her there, then hails a taxi from the other side of the complex. Off she goes to meet her chosen male at a suitable location. Yes, that's how it works, and I've seen it happen. All the women are covered up, of course, so they can't be recognised anyway.

Here's another ruse. Women are allowed to visit other women, so they say they're off to visit lady friends. The driver drops them off at a block of flats, but who is to know where the woman is really going? The driver isn't allowed to go into the woman's home. This is a way round the rules, because in many cases the girls are really seeing their boyfriends.

I heard from friends about another method of meeting. Some men cover themselves up in ladies' black outfits; it sounds a desperate measure, but it's true. A man who's having an affair arrives at the married woman's house and sneaks into the female quarter dressed like a woman, wearing an abaya and accessories. The husband isn't allowed into that area of the house, in case her female friends are visiting and he catches sight of them uncovered. I can't imagine the penalty if a secret lover is apprehended. It would certainly be severe.

Ironically, the prayers I mentioned earlier provide a chance for young men and women to mix. As soon as the call to prayer sounds, people not going to mosques head for benches in the malls. I noticed that young men hang around here and women feel free to talk to them from behind their veils, and if you watch closely you can see telephone numbers being exchanged.

Compared with what I was used to, I found that Arab women have a totally different attitude towards their men. For example, a man might come into the house and rant and rave for some time. The ladies in the room sit quietly during this outburst and just let him get on with it. Often, it blows over and things get back to normal.

No one shouted in my family back home in Denmark all those years ago. If we had a disagreement, we'd sit down and talk about it. So, when T came into the house and shouted at everyone, I was perplexed. The traditional response is for the Arab woman to accept it, but I just couldn't. I know it's not the done thing, but I argued back. One argument led to another, then to another, but I couldn't just sit there and take it.

The woman may not have much power in everyday life, but what she has she uses in the bedroom. Imagine a highly sexed Arab gent coming home, knowing that he alone has access to the mystery behind the veil. He may start his advances, but at a key stage the lady might mention some furniture that's needed, or perhaps some decorating in the front room, or maybe she needs some jewellery. That's the time she can make her husband make promises; once they're made, she carries on with the lovemaking.

There are internet cafes everywhere but, like the gyms, they cater only for men. I eventually found one in Jeddah which had a ladies' section, but only after a search of the entire city.

Saudi is a car enthusiast's dream. Motors come in all shapes and sizes: massive American models, Rolls-Royces,

Jaguars and enormous 4x4s with blacked-out windows. Money is no object for the richer Saudi men, and it seemed to me that they always had the latest models. Women aren't allowed to drive, so I took taxis, using the seating arrangement I described earlier.

I tried to find out why women couldn't drive, as it seemed a bit daft. They've been banned from taking to the roads since 1990. When I asked around, I was told it was mainly a safety issue. You can't see much through the black veil, and I can see the sense in that. Also, I was told, it might encourage women to take their veils off, and that would attract the attention of the religious police.

I was intrigued by all this, and thought that maybe women should get together and protest about the driving issue. I found out, though, that there had been a demonstration in Riyadh in the 1990s. Apparently, a group of nearly 50 women gathered in a supermarket car park, asked their chauffeurs to leave and then drove through the town in convoy. Now these women were no fools – many were academics – and they knew only too well the penalties for wrongdoers.

They were arrested by the Mutaween and there were demands for their beheading. The women and their male relatives were accused of renouncing Islam, for which the penalty is death. The episode was investigated by a commission, which concluded that the women hadn't broken any religious law. They'd gone against tradition, but that was all. During the time of the Prophet Muhammad, women would lead camels through the desert. These could be described as vehicles of the day. Also, before 1990, Bedouin women drove their tribes' pick-ups.

I complied with many of the laws, to make sure that I stayed in the country, and foreigners are under particular pressure to do so. But I must also say that the Saudis are hospitable and dignified people. They are not normally offended by a social mistake that comes from ignorance. When you're living there, you just pick things up very quickly. For example, if you have business to discuss, it can't be mentioned until tea or coffee is poured. It's a sign of bad manners to discuss your sales plan until you're enjoying your drink. Also, the culture involves a lot of personal contact and exchange of small favours, much more than I've ever encountered in the West.

Each time I visited I took my camera with me. I had been told that taking pictures wasn't allowed, but, in my experience, anyone wishing to take a picture of someone should simply ask their permission first. However, no one may take pictures of women. When you look around the big stores, you'll see women used in adverts, but their faces are blacked out. And their bodies are completely covered.

Everyone there has a mobile phone, but camera phones are banned, and if the Mutaween spot you using one they take it and put a pen through the lens. However, you can buy camera phones under the counter in Saudi shops, but, if you have to take one back for any reason, they'll never admit to having sold it to you, so you can forget the guarantee.

I heard on good authority that sometimes, if women fall out, they take secret pictures of each other and post them on the internet. Just imagine the trouble that must cause; breaking all the rules in front of a worldwide audience.

Photographers must be careful about taking a picture of any building in case it offends anyone. Again, it's a case of being discreet and quietly blending in. It's a case of 'when in Rome' and checking the rules.

Before I set out for Saudi Arabia, I learned to check all my baggage. I had no need to take religious books or material, obscene literature or videos, or any pictures of scantily clad women. Obviously, alcohol and drugs are on the banned list, but I always double-checked for anything that might contain pork, or any prescribed drug that might be banned. A traveller carrying a non-approved pill, even in good faith, can be detained.

I need to point out the difference between Saudi Arabia and other Arab countries. As I've said before, the Saudis take a hard-line approach when it comes to women. Religious leaders are always trying to impose further restrictions. They're constantly demanding stricter applications of Islamic law.

In my opinion, it would be hard to go much further. Religious TV and radio programmes already take up most of the airtime. Articles in the press which criticise Saudi Arabia, the Royal Family or Islam are forbidden. Any feature on sex, Judaism, Israel or any other unsuitable subject won't get past the censors.

In magazines, any sections which might be considered offensive are torn out. These will be foreign publications, which are carefully vetted and checked for any adverts mentioning pork products or alcohol. Any picture of a woman is torn out unless it meets strict regulations.

There is a way round this, of course. I knew friends who bought a magazine with the missing pages, then arranged to have the controversial sections faxed to them from other countries. That is breaking the law big time.

The internet has made it much more difficult for the

Saudis to control what people see. Also, with satellite TV, people can watch what they want, and I don't know how the censors can counter this.

People have asked me whether my sons were subjected to racism either in the UK or in Saudi. I can honestly say they haven't faced any racial abuse in the UK. Maybe if they hadn't changed their names to trendy British ones, the situation would have been different.

In Saudi Arabia, it was a different story. Everywhere there's an underlying hatred of the West, and this is reflected in children's attitudes. My boys were made to feel inferior, because they had a Western mother. Also, my kids don't look fully Arab; they look more Italian or perhaps from another part of Europe.

Here's an example of how my kids were made to feel unwelcome. They went to karate lessons in Jeddah, but the teacher took a dislike to them and kept them at the back of the class. The Saudi children were rewarded for their efforts, but my kids never received any recognition and most of the time were snubbed.

Children in Saudi are brought up to believe they are superior. My kids had problems at school, and also during those karate lessons, because they were mixed race; not the finished article, if you like.

Those are my impressions of Saudi Arabia. It's not all bad. You just have to stick to the rules or, if you bend them, do so in the privacy of your own home.

After my adventures there, though, I've no wish to return. My main ambition is to live happily ever after, beside the sea in my Devon home. God willing, or should I say, Enshalla!

13

A PLEA FOR JUSTICE

Back in England, it took several days to recover from saying those goodbyes at that miserable Saudi flat. Everyone involved in my complicated life was now playing a waiting game. My children were anxiously waiting to see me again; I was waiting for a visa, so that I could work at the international school in Jeddah; and T was no doubt waiting for me to call it a day and give up altogether.

The school told me I'd be teaching English and social studies to primary children. I had no real experience in dealing with that age group, so I spent the summer in England reading relevant books and talking to primary teachers. Nothing, though, could have prepared me for the job that awaited me.

I was allowed to talk to the boys by phone once a week, so for the entire week I built up to that moment. It was too risky to tell T that I was coming back, in case he tried to stop my visa. Would he do that to prevent me seeing my children? I had no doubt that the answer was yes.

It was so hard to talk to the boys and not mention my imminent arrival, but I had to keep everything quiet until the paperwork was completed.

All the loose ends were tied up by September 2003 and, before I knew it, I was back on a plane heading for the desert once more. Things were getting a little tight, in that I was due to start work on the day I arrived. That was the way things worked out with the visa and my starting date.

I felt excited, worried, happy, sad, energetic and tired all in a short space of time. I went through the extremes of those emotions as my aircraft landed in Jeddah with the sunrise. The plane inched its way towards the terminal, and I knew that a new dawn was beginning in my life, too.

As I left the aircraft I concealed as much of myself as was practicable. I knew my flowing blonde hair wouldn't be a welcome sight. I checked that my make-up wasn't overdone. Covered from head to toe in traditional dress, I was met by a representative from the school, who eased me through Immigration. It was a mere formality compared with my last experience, when I thought I was going to face a firing squad.

He took me straight to the Dar Jana International School and I started work immediately. I was teaching class 3 boys and class 3 girls, aged nine to ten. In Saudi Arabia, boys and girls are taught separately from year 1. They have separate playtimes and aren't allowed to mix. This segregation continues for the rest of their lives.

Working conditions tested me to the limit. I taught for more than 30 hours a week, with preparation on top of that. I can't criticise the people there, because they merely conformed to the system. Teaching was carried out in an old-fashioned style in bare classrooms.

The children weren't encouraged to be creative. They were used to learning subjects by rote, or off by heart. They simply looked at the blackboard for hours on end and listened to the teacher. The children were also used to being shouted at, and responded to harsh discipline and punishment.

All this, of course, was the total opposite of what I'd been used to in the gentle environment of my Bali school. There we had interactivity with the children. They were loved, so they learned in a completely different way. Their creativity was nourished and grew every day.

In the Saudi school, the children studied art for one hour a week. One aspect of school life I never understood was the unreasonable expectations placed on the children. They had to sit several tests a week. In my classes, the children had their first tests during my first two weeks. They scored 80 per cent or above, and I thought that was really good.

Imagine how I felt when an entire class of girls started to cry. Their mothers expected upwards of 98 per cent in tests; anything less and the mother received grief from the father. That happened because, in Arab countries, the mother is usually responsible for her children's education. If the results aren't excellent, she is considered by her husband to be a failure.

The school imposed a strict dress code on teachers. I had to wear loose clothing that covered me from the neck to the ground. I wore my own clothes, but I had to make sure they covered up all the right places.

The Mutaween would occasionally stand outside to see if we were covered up in our abayas and our hair was also hidden from view. They knew that Western women worked in the school. Any fall in standards could bring a hefty fine for the school and a severe lecture for the unfortunate offender.

I couldn't call these religious policemen attractive. For a start, they all seemed to be short, with large stomachs. They wore traditional white thobes with sandals and black socks, and sported horrible long beards. They also had very loud voices, which they demonstrated by shouting at any lady who dared to show too much femininity.

After my first working day, I was taken to a compound, and that was to be my home for the next 14 months. It consisted of four blocks of flats with a swimming pool in the middle. My flat was on the ground floor.

When I arrived, workmen were still painting and fixing things. There was nothing in the flat except a sofa and two chairs in the living room and two beds in the bedrooms. I called Tina and she sent her driver to pick me up. It was lovely to see her again. She gave me some sheets and kitchen essentials.

I spoke to Abdullah, who told me that my case was entered into the Saudi Royal Court in Jeddah. He was applying for access, so I just hoped and prayed I'd be able to see my boys soon. He explained that we couldn't apply for custody. The Saudi Court would never grant custody of Saudi children to a foreign woman, he said, even if she was the mother of the children.

Abdullah told me to call the boys and tell them the news that I was now in Saudi Arabia, working as a teacher. They were so excited to hear that I was in the country. When I broke the news to T that I was back on the case, he swore and screamed down the phone. He was so angry that I could barely make out what he was saying. Difficult times lay ahead, but I needed my children and they needed me.

Despite my arduous first day, with the flight and then a full teaching schedule, I had homework to do. I had to prepare for the next day, and somehow I managed to work my way through it.

I thought I'd sleep like a log. But, although I was exhausted, I hardly slept. I was worried about my following day at school and how I would cope. It was such an alien environment, but I just had to fit in and make it work. I had no choice, if I wanted to stay in Saudi Arabia.

A bus picked me up at 6.40 in the morning, in time for the 7.20 start. It travelled around the city picking up teachers and students. At 7.30, the students lined up with their teachers in the playground and everyone recited the first verse of the Qur'an. As I'd studied the basics of Islam, I joined in with a dash of confidence.

I was impressed by the headmistress, Mrs Fatin, a short Lebanese lady who oozed authority. In my life, not many people have made me feel obedient and want to stand up straight like a little schoolgirl. I had to be on my toes during class time, because when she went on patrol any flaw in a teacher's technique would be treated as a gaping chasm.

Although the staff were always aware of her presence, and terrified of making mistakes, Mrs Fatin had a compassionate side and supported me. She knew all about my situation, and I think she had a soft spot for me. It helped that she was a former client of Abdullah, who had helped her to win an important case.

I must have made an impression on my first day. Mrs Fatin asked if I would teach the school owner's children privately. This would involve going to his home after school twice a week and teaching English to two of his children. It was good money but, although I needed the work to meet my growing (by the hour, it seemed) legal bills, it was exhausting work.

Also, as my popularity grew I soon had a waiting list for extra tuition. I was the only British teacher at the school, and all the wealthy parents wanted a piece of what I had to offer. I fitted in what I could, but I had to draw a line when it all became too much.

As you can imagine, none of this was going too well with T. It was bad enough for him to accept that I was in the country, getting involved in school life and settling in as much as a blonde European lady can settle into a male-dominated society.

On top of that, he received a summons for a court appearance where the question of access was to be debated. Also, he was receiving letters from my lawyers asking him to help pay my legal bills and to return my jewellery. He wasn't amused.

I managed to concentrate on my job and held everything together, but I still hadn't seen my children since arriving in the country. To make matters worse, the court date for access was three months away because of the necessary paperwork and public holidays.

During those three months, he refused to let me see the boys or even talk to them on the phone, apart from my chats with them during the first week. T went ballistic when he got the letter from the court telling him the date of the hearing. I called to speak to the children and he answered the phone, then started screaming and shouting again. He said that, because I had started my pathetic court action, he wouldn't allow me to see the children until he was ordered to do so.

How could I survive those three months without seeing my children? They were living at the university compound, 40 minutes' drive across Jeddah; so near and yet so very far. The crazy situation preyed on my mind every waking hour.

I came up with a plan. Those all-consuming abayas had other uses, and the main one was disguise. I reckoned that, if I made a totally professional job of covering myself up, no one would recognise me and I could try to see the children.

It worked. My school day finished at about 2.20 in the afternoon. The boys went to the Global International School (similar to my school, Dar Jana) and ended their lessons at 2.30. So I just had time if I hailed a taxi to reach their school and catch a glimpse of them. I knew it would be a painful experience, but what choice did I have? I needed to see their little faces, even if it was only a glimpse.

Imagine how I felt, standing outside their school as T came to pick them up. I was covered up with all the necessary clothing, so I knew I wouldn't be recognised. I just wanted to rip it all off, run over to my boys and take them home with me. But I knew, if I did that, my stay in Saudi Arabia would come to a swift end.

At last, the day of the court hearing arrived. I was to attend a meeting with court staff, who would then make recommendations to the judge. Tina, who'd been to court before, briefed me on what to expect. She also provided me with the upgraded version of the abaya. The abaya can be quite pretty, with tassels, patterns and so on. This one was thick and plain, and in the standard black.

My accessories for the day were black gloves, black socks

and a head cover attached to an overhanging black flap. This could be lifted to reveal my eyes, but in court it had to be in place, to conceal me completely.

I was horrified when I tried it all on. Not one square inch of my body was allowed to be visible. No perfume was allowed; in fact, no trace of femininity at all. That dreaded black flap set the seal on the most dismal outfit I had ever worn in my entire life.

I took a half-day off school for the hearing. My lawyer's assistant, Mr Harlet, picked me up and took me to a large compound in the city centre. I was shown to a women's room with a couple of broken chairs and no air conditioning. I could hardly see out of the black veil. I felt as if I was starting to fry and I feared that I might have a panic attack. Tina had taught me how to put my hand under the veil and get some air inside, so I did that and tried to control my breathing.

My state of helplessness lasted for about half an hour. I felt as if I could pass out at any time, but the thoughts of my children, and why I was in the room at all, somehow managed to keep me going. Just as I felt I was at the limit of what I could bear, and with the temperature in the room now unbearable, Mr Harlet appeared and led me to another room.

To get there, I had to walk through the court buildings, still partially blinded by my head covering. And because my abaya was a little too long, I was worried I might fall over. I arrived in the other room, which contained two desks and three men who looked like religious leaders with their traditional clothing and long beards. The only positive aspect of my new surroundings was the cooler temperature.

The air conditioning seemed to be on, although sweat was running down my body from head to toe.

I was shown to a chair opposite the three religious men. I could just make out the men and their beards, and then became aware of someone else on my right. I peered through the black veil and saw someone adorned from head to toe in traditional Arab costume. To my horror, I realised it was T.

If I was fearful earlier, now I was close to panic. I had no idea he was going to be there. The source of all my pain and anguish was sitting just a few feet from me. There he was, I imagined, gloating at my humiliation. For a few seconds I was happy to be covered up.

As I tried to maintain my concentration, another man appeared and sat next to me. He also wore traditional dress and had a long beard. One of the three men opposite then spoke to me in perfect English. He said the new arrival was a translator. The man with perfect English introduced himself as Mr Matook and then confirmed my name and other personal details. He did the same with T, although this time it was in Arabic and I understood only part of the conversation.

Mr Matook asked more questions of T, who answered in an emotional voice. I suddenly realised that T could have been saying anything and I couldn't join in, agree or disagree, or have any say at all. I decided to raise my hand.

'Excuse me,' I said as loudly as I could through my thick veil. 'I don't understand what's going on here. Could these proceedings be conducted in English?'

Everyone in the room ignored me and continued to talk in Arabic. I was confused, bewildered and close to crying. I felt tears running down my cheeks, although it would have been hard to tell because I was sweating so much.

'Excuse me,' I tried again to attract someone's attention. 'I need to know what's going on. I don't understand. This isn't fair.'

Everyone stopped talking and looked at me. I shuddered as the room fell silent and I felt several pairs of eyes looking in my direction.

'She's right,' Mr Matook announced, turning to T. 'This meeting will proceed in English.'

At this point, T, who'd gone to school and university in Britain and then built up his own business there, made a remarkable statement. 'Me no speak English,' he told the meeting.

With those words, he seemed to have forfeited respect and credibility in that courtroom. Everyone looked at him and I knew he had made a horrendous error. He'd dug a huge hole for himself. Perhaps because I was in a state where I didn't know whether to laugh or cry, I did what came naturally. I burst out laughing.

From that point onwards, the religious men turned towards me and wanted to know what I had to say. T was more or less ignored and I could tell that the boot was now on the other foot.

Mr Matook told me what T had said earlier in Arabic. He had demanded that I should see the children only in the horrible flat owned by his family. I'd seen them there on my previous visit; it was certainly no place for a mum and her four kids to enjoy quality time.

'It's an awful place to meet,' I objected loudly.

Mr Matook told me, in no uncertain terms, to be quiet. I calmed down and explained that I lived in a pleasant compound – an ideal place for the children. I also wanted to take them out and about in Jeddah, to go for a meal or maybe even to a fun park.

During the proceedings, I was allowed to give a fair summary of my situation, and I was grateful for that. I was able to explain what had happened in my marriage and how the boys had been abducted. I also lobbed in the fact that the King's brother had issued my visa for my first trip to Saudi – not that I was one for name-dropping, of course.

'I've heard enough,' Mr Matook announced, then got up from his chair. 'I want to see this flat and I want to see what the mother's compound is like.'

Within a few minutes, a bizarre procession headed from the court buildings to the flat, about half an hour's drive away. T led the way in his car. The religious people followed in what I would describe as an old banger. Mr Harlet then followed in his car. I wasn't allowed to travel with any of them, because none was a relative, so I clambered into a taxi.

On the way there, I couldn't stop thinking about the three religious leaders and how they all looked the same with those long beards. I chuckled to myself because they reminded me of a ZZ Top video I'd seen on MTV. I also thought about my kids and how they knew absolutely nothing about my attempts to see them.

The dreaded flats came into view. I remembered how awful they were and thought to myself that surely the religious people wouldn't be impressed. Well, luck was on my side. They had a look around and screwed up their faces. On a normal day, perhaps, the place would have looked OK. On this day, however, builders had been carrying out some work and the flat looked to be in a total mess. There was dust everywhere and mattresses lay around the place. Even the kitchen appliances had been pulled away from the walls.

I remembered as a child seeing a farce on TV starring Brian Rix. Doors were opening and closing everywhere in a house that was in total confusion. Well, T seemed to be playing that role as he ran from room to room, opening and closing doors as he tried to remedy the situation.

The religious leaders took one look and walked out again. I felt a real surge of satisfaction as I realised that maybe, just maybe, they were on my side. Also Mr Matook seemed to be a fair man, and I liked that.

Things were about to become even more farcical, and this time I was the main player. I still could hardly see anything out of my veil and heavy clothes, and I'd been covered up in the stifling heat for several hours. I knew my abaya was too long, but I'd managed to avoid tripping over it all day. My luck ran out and I fell from grace as I plunged headlong down the stairs of the flat.

The entourage appeared to be concerned, with several voices asking if I was all right. They faced a major problem, however. Under no circumstances were they allowed to touch a woman who wasn't related. I managed to stumble to my feet, battered and bruised. My veil was out of place and now I could only make out various shapes with one eye. I didn't know what T thought about my mishap. I couldn't see him.

Our procession meandered off again, with the same line-up as before, apart from T, who left for home. We drove again through the crowded streets of Jeddah and arrived at my compound. The Saudi owner was there and had what appeared to be a friendly chat with the religious leaders.

These three went inside and examined my flat. They looked satisfied and relaxed as they left. I was astonished when Mr Matook gave me his mobile number and said I should call him if I had any concerns over any aspect of my case. He said they were going back to the office to make a recommendation to the judge, and a court date would be arranged. That hearing, I knew, would decide the outcome of my battle to see my children.

I was overwhelmed by a sense of relief as the cars drove off. I needed to take a shower. My heavy clothes were wringing wet after the trials and tribulations of a long day. I've never enjoyed a shower so much.

A week later, I was back in court, wearing my usual disguise, to hear the judge's decision. I had to sit at the back of a huge room. Further forward, I could just make out my lawyer, T's lawyer and a judge with an assistant. The lawyers spoke in turn; they were ordered out and called back in again. The judge read out a statement, but I had no idea what he was saying.

Only when I got back in the taxi, and my lawyer called me, did I know what the ruling was. The judge had decided that I should have access to my children 24 hours a week, from Thursday evening until Friday evening. Those days are equivalent to a weekend in England. I could see the boys anywhere in Jeddah, although I wasn't allowed to leave the city. I was ecstatic; I laughed and then I wept.

I knew a whopping legal bill would be heading in my direction, but I couldn't care less. I felt like the luckiest mother alive, even if my crumb of comfort was 24 hours a week with the kids.

14

IN ALEX'S OWN WORDS

The events I've just described were, of course, having a profound and disturbing effect on my children. When they were taken away, Max and Alex were ten, Zak was eight and Adam was five.

Alex is the most emotional of my boys. He didn't want to hurt me; nor did he want to hurt his dad. It was very hard for him, coming to terms with being separated from one of his parents. He's a very loyal boy, who shows his affection even during the most difficult of times.

What was it like for the children living in Saudi? They went through the ultimate in culture shocks. One day they were playing happily, blessed with every freedom in the world; the next they were being shouted at. They were being taught lessons in a language they didn't understand. And when they cried no one could hear them.

In his own words, Alex describes some of his experiences:

'I was used to my small school in Bali, where the teachers could talk to us one by one. Everyone was friendly and happy.

'The main problem facing us was the fact that we didn't speak or write Arabic. We also had to learn from the Qur'an. We all sat in rows looking at a blackboard, and I didn't have a clue what was going on.

'After school my dad made us study for four hours a day to try to catch up. It was just so hard, and I couldn't understand why I was so young and having to go through all this. Dad was getting stressed out trying to teach the four of us, and he shouted and hit us on the back of the head if we didn't understand. I'm not proud to say that, but that's what happened to each of us.

'We made some friends at school, but some of the others bullied us a bit because we weren't real Saudis. They didn't see us as full Arabs, because we were mixed race. I don't know why, but everyone seemed to think we were Americans.

'Everything was so different to Bali. Sometimes I would wake up on a Saturday morning and wonder where Mum was. I would think that she might be able to take us to the pictures. Then I remembered Saturday was a school day here, and there were no cinemas.

'I asked Dad a lot about Mum, because she was supposed to be following us from Bali. He told us how horrible she was, and how we should have nothing to do with her, and we should stop asking. We were all confused, because Mum had always been good to us and made nice meals and drinks. Most of all, we missed snuggling up with her and listening to her stories.

'After a while, we realised that Mum wasn't coming. We guessed that, if she was going to appear, she'd have to come uninvited and track us down.

'We were so happy when she came over for the first time. We had to see her in an awful flat and we had to live there sometimes as well. I didn't like the place because when we first arrived we stayed with Uncle Adnan and that was a nice house. We saw Mum three times a week in there. She always came with lots of presents and Dad was swearing a lot. I don't think Dad or our uncle expected her to make it into Saudi Arabia. I knew my mum better than that!

'Later, when she came back to work as a teacher, she went to the court and we saw her at her compound. That was great because when her driver picked us up we could go anywhere in Jeddah. She took us shopping and bought us Game Boys and clothes. She spent lots of money on us. One thing we weren't happy about was that we could only see her once a week and we were all so sad when we came to the end of our 24 hours.

'We were always saying goodbye to Mum. Dad was always grumpy when he picked us up. It was hard for my little brother, Adam, because, when he cuddled Mum to say goodbye, he wouldn't let go of her. He was getting totally confused and I remember him holding on and holding on to Mum. It was horrible, really horrible and the whole thing was getting like a bad dream.

'After Mum's first visit, it was hard for us to say goodbye. We weren't allowed to say goodbye at the

*airport. We had to say goodbye at the flat. My brothers
were crying but I didn't cry. I just looked at Mum's face
and I knew she was coming back. She winked at me
and that said it all.'*

15

LOVE IN THE DESERT

What a result. What a day. A Saudi court coming down on the side of a woman? A *foreign* woman? It beggared belief, and I made a mental note of everyone I had to thank as I gulped in the cool air from the taxi's air conditioning. Close to the top of my list was a rather special someone called Jamil.

I hadn't expected to find love in the desert. I wasn't looking for any. I was there to find my children and bring them home. Love did seek me out, and it found me.

The longer I stayed in Saudi Arabia, the more I discovered that people did lead secret lives, away from the prying eyes of the religious police. There was an underworld of clandestine relationships, porn, drugs and alcohol. I was stunned to discover that most of the people indulging in all this were Saudis.

I became friendly with several Saudi men and women, and was astonished to find out that many of them were having affairs; by 'affair', I mean that a single man could be carrying on with a single girl, outside the recognised system.

It is true that the more something is banned or forbidden, the harder people will try to seek out this forbidden fruit. On the surface, it all seems literally black and white, with the dreary dark clothes of the women and the shining thobes worn by the men. Underneath, there is a rich tapestry of colour – prohibited, banned, illegal – but it's there, and thriving.

Jamil was Lebanese, 26 years old and a Christian. He was the same age as George, my lover in Bali. The big difference was that, in Bali, George and I could do what we liked. We could go out for a meal, hold hands and even kiss in public. I met Jamil in Saudi Arabia, hardly a breeding ground for young lovers.

Memories of George, the tall South African, had long since faded. Now, in Saudi, I was working so hard to get my children back and I didn't think I would become involved in another relationship. It happened, and I have no regrets about it.

Jamil had big brown eyes and wore a constant smile. He looked so young and I was flattered that another man in his twenties found me attractive. He was always cracking jokes and thought, like me, that some of the country's laws were ludicrous. Jamil was only there to earn money, because back home in Lebanon he would have received a fraction of his Saudi salary.

I found living in Saudi Arabia so difficult that Jamil became my escape route. I was so lonely without the children, family and all my own friends. I did make some new friends, such as Tina, but, oh, how I missed everyone else.

Jamil helped to ease my feelings of loneliness. Had I not met him, I doubt if I could have survived in such an alien environment. Secretly, I knew he was always there, and he provided a sense of normality in a crazy world. If I had a bad day in court, he was there; if I had a disaster at work, he was there; if I felt down, I knew he was there for me.

He was my secret rock, and no one knew about him; not even my lawyer, not even my best friends. Any whiff of our affair and the religious police would have been on to us. It would have meant that my achievements in the country so far would have counted for absolutely zero.

Jamil worked for a computer company. I never found out exactly what he did. I think he wrote programs and installed them, but all I know is that he was a genius with computers. If my laptop went wrong, he could sort it out straight away.

I sort of bumped into Jamil. He used to take the teachers from my compound on shopping trips. The alternative was going by taxi, which always proved to be a hassle. You had to walk to the main road and hail one, then haggle over the price. Many women were attacked by taxi drivers when I was there, so Jamil provided a valuable and safe service for us single girls.

Of course, Jamil wasn't allowed to drive a single, unrelated woman anywhere. That was one of the laws I had to get used to. Just to survive, I had to break some of them most of the time. We just hoped we wouldn't be stopped by the dreaded Mutaween.

The teachers, me included, were taking a chance because a roadblock would have put me on the road to big trouble. I never knew if anyone got caught, but we lived in constant fear of being found out.

205

I don't think beheading or cutting bits off was an option, but we'd have received a severe telling-off from the religious police. If the Mutaween had wanted to make an example of anyone, they could do whatever they wanted.

I think I was a bit in love with Jamil. I thought he was attractive and gorgeous, and so young and fresh. He was always laughing and we joked together about the bizarre system in Saudi. We wondered what would happen if we strolled through the shopping malls in Jeddah, hand in hand, with our beachwear on. I think the Mutaween would all have had heart attacks and put us on the first plane out of there.

I surprised myself by going out with Jamil. I was so off men. After what happened to my relationship with T, I simply hated the male population. And in Saudi, as you don't talk to men anyway, I accepted that I should be on my own in my quest to get my children back.

The reason I bumped into Jamil was that he knew another teacher, Sarah, who lived in our flat. She was also Lebanese, and Jamil liked to spend some time with her because they knew each other from home. Jamil lived in another part of the compound, so he became a familiar face.

Sarah was married and waiting for her family to join her in Saudi Arabia. When they eventually arrived from Lebanon, they all moved into another house and I had the flat to myself for nine months. When she was living there with me, Jamil often knocked at the door on his way out shopping, to ask if she needed anything. I often answered the door, and to begin with I was really short with him; he was a man and I didn't want to talk to any men, viewing them all as my enemies.

I said, 'Sarah isn't here at the moment and I don't need anything.' Most of the time I shut the door in his face.

'You were rude to me at your front door a few days ago,' Jamil told me off later as I sat, reflecting on my life, beside the pool in the compound. I was only half listening, as I was intrigued by his enormous brown eyes. Several people from the compound had gathered for a coffee, but I was only interested in those eyes.

'Sorry, I didn't mean to be rude,' I said. 'I'm not thinking about much apart from my kids at the moment. Nothing else matters.'

As I offered up my explanation, I studied Jamil more closely. When I managed to avert my gaze from his eyes, I could see he was in all-round good condition. Yes, he was gorgeous.

As I talked to him, I remembered how I'd felt with George in Bali. Again, I was overcome with a rush of something; maybe it was a mix of adrenalin and pure passion. Perhaps I was attracted to his typical Lebanese appearance, the twinkle in his eyes or his athletic body. I reckon it was a combination of everything. God, I fancied him like mad.

'Hey, how do you keep so fit?' I asked, flirting more than a little. 'You must go to a gym, to have muscles like those.' I surprised myself with my boldness.

'There's a gym in the compound,' he replied. 'You may not have seen it, because it's in a disused flat. Anyone can use it, though. It's Friday tomorrow. I'm off work, so you must be off as well.'

'You're going to lead me astray on such a holy day in Saudi,' I teased. 'You should be at the mosque tomorrow ...'

'I'm a Christian,' he butted in. 'So we won't be going to

any mosque. You can go, if you feel that way inclined. I'm going to the gym.'

I felt another surge of excitement as Jamil arranged to come round at noon the next day. I decided not to close the door in his face ever again.

The following day, I woke up earlier than normal, still with the children completely on my mind but with some gentle thoughts of Jamil too. I wondered if our gym session would lead to anything. I concluded that if we started seeing each other it would give me something else to think about. Then I thought I'd just be using him. Damn, I wasn't thinking straight at all.

I lay there trying to put my thoughts in some semblance of order before easing myself out of bed and into my as yet unworn gym clothes. I was ready for a new chapter in my life and, at twelve o'clock, right on cue, there was a rat-a-tat-tat on the door. I looked through the spy hole and could see my gorgeous gym instructor waiting for me.

When I opened the front door, Jamil gave me a gentle peck on the cheek. I followed him to another building in the compound and, sure enough, in an empty flat, there were some antiquated weights and a collection of running and rowing machines. They were the oldest and most worn-out contraptions I'd ever seen, but they served a dual purpose; they helped with my fitness and they played Cupid in my imminent relationship with Jamil.

'This is how to use the rowing machine properly,' Jamil said, demonstrating as he flexed his muscles and the equipment lurched into life. I watched intently, then climbed aboard and rowed at a tiny fraction of his pace. He showed me how everything worked, and how to stay safe and uninjured. Half an hour was enough for me and then I thought it was time for a heart-to-heart chat with my new admirer. We went back to my flat for a coffee.

'I don't know what you've heard about me,' I began. 'I know you live here to make some money. My children were stolen and I'm here to get them back. I'm sorry that I'm sometimes happy and I'm sometimes sad. I have OK days, bad days, terrible days and disastrous days.'

'Stolen?' His head leaned to the side and his expression became more and more quizzical as I related my story.

'Well, I say "stolen". You could say "kidnapped", or "abducted". At any rate, they were taken from our home in Bali by my husband. At first, I couldn't see them; now I get the chance to see them occasionally. I'm trying to get them back and it's a horrific legal battle. I just thought I'd fill you in.'

Jamil paused for a moment and looked at the floor, assembling a list of complicated facts into an ordered sequence inside his head.

'My friend Sarah said you didn't have your kids,' he said. 'I didn't realise things were as bad as this. To be honest, I can't imagine a woman having any chance of achieving anything by going to court in Saudi. I didn't even know women were allowed to go to court.'

'I know, I get treated like a dog in there,' I muttered. 'But I'm going to keep trying, keep chipping away at the legal system. It's all I can do. My children are my life.'

Jamil didn't say anything for several minutes. He looked at the floor and stroked his chin, then his smile returned. 'I'll help you,' he offered, getting up from his chair. 'I can't be seen to have anything to do with you, but I reckon I can give you some support, even if it's just some advice and encouragement. Hope that's OK?'

'I'm up for that,' I said with relief, though at the same time I wondered if it might all be too much for him. Many men would have abandoned me, especially in a country where he was risking his future even talking to a single woman.

For three weeks, we continued going to the gym and chatting. Often it was tempting to ask him to stay. Sometimes I fancied hugging and kissing him. Jamil was a real gentleman and when our evenings ended he left when he felt the time was right. I believe he sensed that, at night, all I wanted was to be with my children; that wasn't possible, so I needed to be alone with my thoughts.

During those three weeks of flirting, we both knew that a mutual attraction was growing. One evening we were eating a takeaway and watching a movie. George must have started a trend back in Bali, as this combination seemed to get me going.

Jamil turned to me, took my hand and told me I was beautiful. 'I've wanted to tell you this for some time,' he said with a nervous pitch to his voice. 'Everything about you is so attractive and I've been wanting to hold you and kiss you for ages. I so, so much want to make love to you.'

Although my face was tanned, I felt it turning a bright red as one of my familiar flushes came and went. I remember the same thing happening with George. I had fancied George and now I fancied Jamil like crazy.

I moved off to the bedroom first, again surprised that I was taking the lead. I undid my top. Jamil could see I wasn't wearing a bra, so he took full advantage; not that I was putting up much of a fight. What happened next was amazing. We'd been holding back for three weeks and now all our feelings overflowed. It was an extraordinary session, full of passion and caring. For those few moments, I wasn't worried about deportation, stoning or even beheading. I had a physical need and it was being met in full.

'We mustn't tell a soul about this,' Jamil whispered when we'd finished. I was worried about the noise we'd made. 'We have to keep it a complete secret, otherwise we'll be in big trouble.'

The consequences were all too clear to me too. Any slip-up and the religious police would have a field day. I agreed that no one should know.

We kept up our routine until I left the country. On a typical day, Jamil would come to my flat around ten in the evening after finishing work. He'd take me to the seafront in his car and we'd just walk and talk. It was great to get out of the flat, but even better to see Jamil. I had loads of time on my hands because, although I was teaching, I saw the children just once a week.

That's where Jamil was worth his weight in gold. He would always make sure that he was at the compound at five o'clock on Fridays after my allotted 24 hours with the kids. I couldn't go back into the flat for at least an hour after they'd left. Their toys were still there and the remnants of our lovely weekend lay scattered throughout the flat. Jamil always took me out shopping, or for a walk, to prepare me for going back to the flat.

We both knew the affair would come to an end if I won my custody battle. I couldn't see Jamil jetting off to England with the children and me. We also knew that it might end if

I didn't win custody. Wherever the children went, he knew I'd be following.

In the end, I did follow the children under bizarre circumstances, and I had to leave Jamil behind.

To this day, I can't thank him enough. Jamil really was my rock in the desert.

16

TOGETHER AGAIN

I decided to call Jamil with news of my access order as soon as I could. The impact of my relatively successful Saudi court session was still sinking in. I just sat there in the taxi, sweating under my heavy black outfit and felt myself starting to shake.

I should have been sitting as far away from the male driver as possible, but I forgot about that custom and he didn't push it. He couldn't see any of me but he could sense I'd been through the mill.

'Sorry,' I whimpered, 'I'm just trying to get myself together.'

I bowed my head, bit my lip and tried to snap out of it. I knew I should be happy, as the court had backed me. My attempt at positive thinking worked. I knew that four dear faces were about to play a crucial role in my life once more.

For an average mum, it's easy to take everything for granted. You can have a meal with the kids; take them shopping; you can even take them to the movies. None of those options was available to me. Not yet, anyway. A slightly brighter future seemed possible, though. I forced myself to realise that I should be celebrating, rather than going over and over old ground. OK, I'd have been happier with more than 24 hours a week, but that's what they'd given me.

For a rash moment, I pictured a glass of champagne. Well, the alcohol laws would have knocked that plan on the head. I couldn't take off my all-black clothing either, but that could wait. I felt my mood changing for the better. And I did need to do some celebrating. I asked the driver to take me to Tina's compound.

Tina organised a coffee, a cigarette, a swim in the pool and a takeaway pizza. She also helped me to plan for my first legal reunion with my children. It was to be a 24-hour get-together, from Thursday evening until Friday evening, as ordered by the court. And those glorious few hours were only two days away.

So what was I going to do with them? Where was I going to take them? What options were available?

I wondered what would be feasible in the time available, to satisfy all four of my boys. I decided that we would have a home-cooked 'Mummy meal' on the Thursday evening at my flat, and take it from there.

I counted the hours, then the minutes, until Thursday afternoon arrived. Not long to go now, I told myself. The phone rang at three o'clock. It was Max.

'Mum, Dad can't take us to see you,' he said. 'Grandma is ill, and he can't come. He says you'll have to come and pick us up. Please come and pick us up. We all love you.'

I couldn't believe it. I went into a panic because I didn't know how to get to T's compound and I lacked transport.

Tina came to the rescue again, lending me her car and driver, and off we went to the other side of Jeddah. It took us almost an hour to get there.

We had agreed that the pick-up point would be one of the entrances to the university. T had said he didn't want me to come to his flat, as I was an unworthy person. As we drew up to the gate, I saw the boys with their backpacks on, looking anxiously down the road. When I got out of the car, they all threw themselves at me and attempted to hug me. I tried to share out the hugs equally as best I could, while we all jabbered and shared our news.

One by one, the boys produced presents for me from their pockets. Adam handed me a piece of paper, folded many times. When I opened it, I could see a letter and a drawing. The letter said he loved me and missed me. The drawing was of a beautiful butterfly.

Next came a warm bar of chocolate from Zak. It was my favourite and I enjoyed every mouthful even though it was more like drinking hot chocolate.

The twins gave me a little bracelet they'd saved up for and bought from their local shop. I put it on at once and felt like the most loved mother in the entire world. I felt as if there was no tomorrow, as if there was nothing beyond our present reunion. I didn't want to know about anything beyond those 24 hours.

Back at my flat, I started to cook the meal, which I'd prepared in advance so as to maximise our time together. A sense of normality filled the flat as the children chilled out, put the television on and enjoyed my special casserole and mashed potato.

We made every second count. After the meal, we went out

with Tina to a funfair and a shopping mall. I splashed out on toys and clothes. I was having a ball. We arrived back home exhausted and all fell asleep together.

The next morning we woke up early, savoured each mouthful of a full English breakfast (excluding bacon) and lazed around the compound. We swam, played, watched a movie and lived our hours to the full. All too soon, our glorious get-together was over, and the boys were gone.

I didn't want to risk a second non-appearance by T, so Tina agreed that her driver should take me to pick up the boys every Thursday. That scheme didn't always go according to plan. One Thursday four o'clock came, then a quarter past. Where was that driver? The phone rang; it was Tina saying the car had broken down. I formed a picture of my children standing beside a dusty road with their backpacks on, waiting for me. They'd waited all week for the moment; I'd waited all week to hug them.

'Shit! What a disaster,' I said as I tried to remember Jamil's mobile number. Was he working today? In my haste, I misdialled the number. I ran to my bedroom, checked the number and redialled. This time I got through and said, 'Jamil, I have a huge problem. Help!' Stammering and stuttering, I told him my predicament. Calling a taxi wasn't an option; by the time one arrived and I'd explained where I wanted to go, it would be too late.

'I'll take you,' were the words I so wanted to hear. 'My car's outside the compound. I'll be there in a minute.'

The journey normally took about an hour. Jamil did it in 35 minutes, breaking the speed limit all over the place. We got away with it and arrived at the university just five minutes late.

Afterwards, though, I received a stern lecture from my lawyer. Abdullah said that, if T had found out about an unlicensed driver taking me to pick up the children, the consequences didn't bear thinking about. Before all future visits, I checked the roadworthiness of Tina's car and found a reliable taxi driver as a standby.

I spent Christmas 2003 and saw in the New Year in Saudi, wondering what lay in store for me during the year ahead. In my flat I'd put up some Christmas decorations, but I kept them well hidden. The Saudi authorities frown on any overt display of Christianity, although if you celebrate in private you should be left alone. I didn't want to get into any trouble, so I spent Christmas alone behind closed curtains.

Unfortunately, my access hours didn't coincide with Christmas Day. My thoughts were of the festive season in the UK and all the children who were enjoying being with their families. My kids were stuck here in a foreign land, not allowed to join in the festivities and separated from their mum.

In fact, I knew that my children were very unhappy because in the spring of 2004 they ran away from T's house. On a Wednesday evening, just before a two-week religious holiday, I'd finished teaching and was at home, having a snooze on the sofa and looking forward to my normal access arrangements the next day. Suddenly, my doorbell woke me with a start. To my complete surprise, Max, Alex and Zak were standing outside my door. They were all grinning and wearing backpacks.

They came in and told me they couldn't stand living with their father any more. He was always in a terrible mood, they were forced to do so many household chores and they'd simply had enough. So, while he was giving Adam hours of homework, they chose their moment and made a break for it.

I knew I had to play everything by the book, make all the right moves, so I picked up the phone and called T. I asked him if he knew the three boys' whereabouts. He told me they were playing outside.

'They're not,' I said. 'They're with me. They've run away from you.'

He screamed back that I was a bitch and had told them to leave him. Of course, I'd done nothing of the sort. He said it was my responsibility to get the children back to him – now!

The conversation grew more and more heated. I felt I was within my rights to ask why the children had left. How were they being treated? How was he looking after them? I said I wouldn't send them back until I knew why they'd left.

I needed legal advice, so I called Abdullah and told him what had happened. He advised me to keep the boys with me and said that Adam would have to join me the next day, to comply with the access agreement.

That was unlikely to happen, I thought, and I was right. I left the three boys with Tina and went off with her driver to pick up Adam at five o'clock. T didn't come with him to the university gate; in fact, there was not a soul to be seen.

The security guards told me T had instructed them not to let anyone through to see Adam. I was upset because I knew that my son was inside, totally confused and probably crying his eyes out.

I called Abdullah again on my mobile and explained the situation. He said I should go back to Tina's compound and he would sort it all out. It was hard for me to turn round and leave without my child and I felt tearful all the way back.

Abdullah's wife, Kathy, was at Tina's compound to greet me on my return. She was chatting to my other children and Tina. Abdullah was nowhere to be seen. They wouldn't tell me where he'd gone and they seemed a bit secretive.

About three hours later – with me still none the wiser – there was a loud knock on the door. It was Abdullah, carrying in his arms a sleepy-looking Adam wrapped in a blanket. I just hugged my youngest boy, while Abdullah stood and watched with a wide grin.

He told me that he'd gone with the police to T's flat and laid down the law. Showing him the court order, he'd told T in the clearest of terms that the court would take an extremely dim view of any attempt to prevent Adam's weekly visit. After three hours of negotiations, T allowed my confused boy to leave with Abdullah.

During those three hours, Adam had kept himself busy. He'd drawn a butterfly that opened up to reveal more lovely pictures. He handed it to me with pride and a big smile.

The boys told me they had no intention of going back to their father. We were all on school holiday for two weeks, so why couldn't they stay? I was their mum, so why on earth not?

We decided that Max, the eldest, would call his father. I heard him pleading with T to allow them just to spend some time with me. I was sitting a few feet away, but I could hear T screaming and shouting down the phone. He warned the boys that they had to return after the weekly visit, otherwise there would be huge trouble.

I called Abdullah for more advice and he suggested that I should keep the children for the holiday and just go off somewhere. We were breaking the court order, but he said he was sure that the judge would take the circumstances into account.

Tina had the use of a flat at an exclusive beach resort just outside Jeddah. She suggested that we should all go there; she didn't need to ask me twice.

Within an hour, we were on our way by car. Sometimes in life, I think you have to take chances and risks. This was my chance to enjoy some quality time and really connect with my children again.

The compound was completely Westernised, although without the alcohol, of course. There were hundreds of villas, flats, shops, a marina and gorgeous beaches beside the Red Sea. The flat had stunning views, and I just compared it with that awful dump where the boys and I had had our first meetings.

We swam, ate, laughed and joked, cooked together, played cards, watched television and enjoyed long walks. In no time at all, the sun had set on our fabulous holiday. I wanted it to never end – with good reason, as things turned out.

Back at my flat after our break, I called T to ask him if I should bring the children over. He didn't answer his mobile, which surprised me as he'd sent dozens of texts while we were away.

The situation was becoming even more complicated. The children were due back at their school, the Global International, the next day and I couldn't get hold of T. I rang his mobile constantly and got no reply. I tried his brother, but with no success there either.

All I could do was to take my children to school myself. The boys had no uniforms or books with them, but when I just showed up with them the staff were sympathetic and said they could stay.

Fortunately, the school where I taught had a few extra days off, and that meant I could arrange to have the boys taken and collected by taxi.

There was an unexpected drama, though, on the second day. I'd left Adam with another family at the compound because he had a cold, and I'd taken the three others to school. On arriving in the taxi to pick them up in the afternoon, I was greeted by some rather sombre-looking members of staff. They said the three boys had been collected by their father. Not only that, they told me he'd been shouting like a man possessed. To keep the peace, they'd let him take them away.

The head teacher at the boys' school, Mrs Mahra, had some bad news for me. Under no circumstances, she said, would they be allowed back there after T's outburst. I couldn't really argue with that. In her position, I would have done the same thing.

As soon as I arrived back at the flat, I called T's house. Max answered, as he'd been told to, because T wouldn't speak to me. In the background, I could hear the other children crying as their father screamed instructions to him.

Max had to tell me everything was my fault and, if the boys were to go to another International School, I would have to pay all the fees. It's not hard to imagine the state I was in, because my children and I were being punished just for wanting to spend some time together.

In my opinion, T had managed to get out of paying the school fees and was meting out punishment at the same time. I thought the situation suited him down to the ground.

I had no option but to call the head teacher at my school to see if the boys could enrol there. Not a problem, said my wonderful boss, Mrs Fatin. Also, because I had four children, and I worked there, I was in line for a decent discount. Every little helped, as my expenses were building up to a worrying amount. T didn't object to the new arrangements.

With the boys now at my school, it was wonderful to be able to see them so often. I wasn't teaching them personally, but each time I had a break I sneaked off to meet them.

On the access front, I managed to earn a two-hour bonus. I was obviously in T's good books because I'd paid the school fees. He took the boys to lessons every day and picked them up afterwards. When Thursday came, he allowed me to take them home at three instead of the agreed five o'clock, and that cheered me up a bit.

I found out that T wasn't on the best of terms with his new wife, Iman. She was using Abdullah as her lawyer, as her family had been impressed with his efforts in securing my access agreement in the Saudi court.

I was intrigued to hear about Iman. I thought I should meet her and compare notes. It seemed that we had both made the same mistakes and ended up in the same boat. Abdullah called Iman and gave her my number. Several hours later, my phone rang and a polite, well-spoken voice addressed me in almost-perfect English. It was Iman's brother. He said he was making contact because Iman didn't speak good English. We talked for about 45 minutes, and he told me about the family's long list of issues with T. One of these was the name for their first baby. Iman had wanted to call the new child after her mother. However, T went to the hospital and registered the baby in his own mother's name. Iman was furious.

Her brother – who worked for the Saudi airline – invited me over to Iman's family home, owned by her parents. It was time to meet the new wife, although how long she retained that status remained to be seen.

Two days later, Tina's driver picked me up and I was on my way through the busy streets of Jeddah. We drew up outside a large, imposing house. I could see that I was visiting a well-to-do family.

I was greeted by a maid, who took my abaya and showed me into a splendid reception room on the ground floor. There, waiting to meet me, were Iman's two brothers and her mother, Miriam. They were friendly and polite, so soon I was sitting chatting with them and feeling at ease.

I heard footsteps and then a pleasant-looking, smiling woman in her mid-thirties entered the room, carrying a beautiful baby girl.

'I am pleased to meet you,' she said, looking at me intently. 'I am Iman.'

The child's resemblance to T was astonishing. She had the same thick, black, curly hair and dark-brown eyes. I wasn't sure what to call the baby because of the dispute over names. Iman explained in broken English that, although T had officially called her after his mother, she and her family called the child Miriam, after her own mother, and that was how they planned to continue.

It was like looking into T's eyes. Little Miriam smiled and a tiny hand reached out for me. Iman passed her to me. I was holding my boys' half-sister and I started to feel quite emotional. Before I could burst into tears, a maid appeared and gently took the child from my grasp.

'The baby is tired and needs to go to sleep,' the maid told me in Arabic.

My schoolgirl grasp of the language was up to the job, and I said goodbye to little Miriam.

Another maid appeared with a tray containing Arabian coffee, served in tiny cups, and a selection of tasty-looking cakes. The brother I'd spoken to on the phone began to tell me about their family's encounter with T. He said everyone loved my boys, and they used to spend some time at the house. At first, he said, everyone felt sorry for T, as he was a single father with four boys to bring up. T had told them how bad I was, that I had endless affairs, never took care of my children and was a useless mother and wife. The brother said they didn't like the way T was treating the boys. They thought he was harsh with them, and added that they would benefit from some new clothes and shoes.

Iman said that when she married T and moved into his house she replaced most of the boys' old clothes. I liked her at once. I felt grateful that she'd looked after the boys so well. I did feel a bit jealous when she talked about how fond she was of Adam. She said he'd given her a little box of drawings.

I didn't want to overstay my welcome so, after about an hour, I decided it was time to leave. Everyone said they wanted to see me again, so I arranged to come over the following weekend.

When I arrived for that next visit, I was shown upstairs to a large open-plan sitting area. Iman's sister was there with her two children and other members of the family. We played with the children and talked mostly about T's behaviour. The entire family seemed to be furious with him.

The household was religious and traditional. When it was time for evening prayer, Miriam opened the window so that we could hear the call to prayers at the local mosque. She said her husband was leading the prayers. Everyone except the maids and I took part in the proceedings.

Shortly afterwards, a feast of Arab food arrived; the family certainly knew how to entertain. After I'd eaten all I could, it was time for shopping. Iman, her sister and I put on our abayas and one of the brothers drove us to the shops. I chuckled when I imagined what T would think about his two wives going shopping together. After we'd had a good look round and a coffee, I took a taxi back to my flat.

The third and final time I met Iman was at my compound. About a week after our shopping trip, her brother dropped her off outside. It was difficult to talk because her English was poor and her brother wasn't there to translate.

I made a mistake that day, out of pure ignorance. The boys had told me that T was now looking for a Moroccan wife. I didn't have any feelings left for T, but the situation was still too raw for Iman. I told her what the boys had said and I could see in her eyes that she still loved him.

Iman and T were due in court the next day for a pre-court meeting. There they would speak to one of the religious leaders and he would judge if there was any hope for the marriage.

Arabic women are known to be jealous. And I'd told Iman that T – the only man she'd ever been with and the father of her baby – was thinking of marrying another woman. It was sure to spark a reaction, and what a reaction.

That evening, Abdullah called me to say that Iman was

moving back in with T and had dropped divorce proceedings. Sadly, it wasn't to last. Three weeks later, a distraught Iman went back to her parents. During that brief reunion, however, she became pregnant again.

I still ask myself what would have happened if I'd kept my big mouth shut.

To some people, it might sound that I'm being harsh to T. Some might think that here is a single dad, trying his best with the children, helping them with homework, driving them to and from school and, until now, paying most of their school fees.

All this, though, he seemed to be doing to stay in control and exclude me. I can only tell it as I saw it.

My entire and constant aim was to get the children back to England at virtually any cost. T was comfortable, thinking I would pay all the school fees from then on and that he had me over a barrel.

But his happy days were to end. I wrote him a letter saying I couldn't afford to pay the school fees any more. If he wanted the boys to receive a proper education, he should send them back to England, where they could receive it all for free. This didn't go down too well. His reaction was to tell the children that, if they were to go to an International School in Saudi, their mother would have to leave the country. Otherwise, they would be sent to a normal Saudi religious school, learning Arabic and studying the Qur'an. The children were devastated. They enjoyed the education they received at International Schools, and the thought of the alternative horrified them.

My options played on my mind until the summer holidays arrived. I decided that, in the boys' best interests, I should return to England. I had no choice. I couldn't take the chance that he would put them into a Saudi school. Not only did they not want that, but the prospect of that type of education horrified me too. I also hated the thought of leaving my children again.

I knew I had to return, of course, to resume teaching in September. T believed that I was going to leave the country for good and I was happy with his line of thinking.

When the time came to leave, I packed lots of the boys' belongings. I asked them to tell T that their things were ready to be picked up. He dropped them off to spend a couple of hours with me, and they were so upset. Alex cried and cried, and I thought he was never going to stop. I took advantage of those two hours to go on a final, emotional, shopping trip.

I was due to leave the next day and the children begged T to take them to the airport to say their farewells, as they had no idea when they would see me again.

I wished that T had left little Miriam at home when he brought the boys to the airport. I just wanted my boys to be there. It felt to me that he was showing that he had an extended family, now including a little girl, and my nose was being rubbed well and truly in the mire.

I gave the boys their final cuddles and Alex whispered that he knew I would be back soon. It broke my heart not to say anything about when I would return, as their education depended on my leaving – for good, as far as T was concerned.

In tears, I headed for the departure lounge, and I could see my children's tiny faces gradually disappearing. I knew I was leaving them in unhappy surroundings, in searing 50-

degree heat and, most disturbing of all, without their mother.

I arrived back in England yet again, and stayed with my friend Caroline while I planned my return to Saudi Arabia. I took a break in Denmark to celebrate my fortieth birthday with my family.

Then, like the proverbial bad penny, I turned up again in Saudi to resume my teaching at the International School – where my boys were studying – much to T's horror. I found out when I arrived back that he'd enrolled them there, although the fees were still to be paid. I encountered him as he was waiting to pay them. I walked into the parents' waiting room, and there he was. The look on his face! He thought I was back in England having a miserable time. Yet, here I was, back at work, strolling the school's corridors and looking as determined as ever to reclaim my children.

Having seen me, T didn't pay the fees, of course. He asked for the boys' enrolment papers and told the head teacher that they wouldn't be coming back. He enrolled the two younger boys at another International School and decided to teach the twins at home. I continued teaching at my school, sadly without the boys around.

There was still the matter of my court order, which allowed me to see the children for 24 hours a week. My lawyer called T and asked if they could spend the next weekend with me. T agreed, and I picked up the boys at his compound, as I'd done many times before.

What happened next was quite shocking. The boys and I stayed at Tina's place on the Thursday night. On the Friday morning, we had a lie-in.

I woke up to find that Max and Alex were gone. They'd vanished, with their belongings. I searched inside and outside and called their mobiles, all to no avail. My other two boys were still asleep, so what had happened to the twins?

Well, T had called them early that morning and given them their orders. They were to go to a supermarket near Tina's compound, where he would pick them up. I found out later that he'd promised them a new life in England with him if they would have nothing to do with me. I realised he couldn't cope with me on his trail any longer.

Max called me from T's flat and told me what I didn't want to hear. He said that he and Alex didn't want to stay with me, or even see me any more. Obviously, at that stage he had to keep quiet about England. No way did T want me to know what was going on, or I'd be on his trail again. He desperately needed time in England without my knowing he was there, so that he could get organised and settle in with the twins. He had to find a way to keep me in Saudi. So he left the two little ones there under the custody of Uncle Adnan. Max told me that he, Alex and T were going to Dubai with T's mother so that she could have surgery.

When I told my lawyer this story, he said it was a load of nonsense. He was sure they were all going to England, and told me confidently, 'It's a smokescreen. I think we can see through that one!'

As usual, he was right. The twins left for England with T and his mother.

In fact, Abdullah was able to confirm with Jeddah airport that they'd left for London. It was an extraordinary feeling to know that two of my children were now in England, two were in Saudi Arabia and none of them was living with their mother, despite all my efforts. Life can get complicated!

Abdullah told me that T might send for the two little ones

before long. He made sure that I had an exit visa in my passport so that I could make a rapid departure at any time. It took three weeks to organise, and T knew that, so I thought I'd try to stay ahead of the game.

Ramadan arrived, and with it a horrific experience. I thought I was going to lose my life. Two other teachers had now moved into my flat. I wasn't fasting and neither was one of the other teachers. Remember that, during Ramadan, anyone snacking or even chewing gum in a public place can be arrested.

One Thursday morning, we were preparing schoolwork and took some coffee out to the swimming pool. This was a private area, so it didn't fall under the restrictions on fasting. We noticed a strange, furtive-looking man going out of the gate. He didn't leave, though, but merely appeared again, from another part of the compound. He was watching us.

Later, while I was out doing some private teaching, the same man climbed through an open window into the bedroom next to mine and threatened one of my flatmates with a pair of scissors. He demanded to know about me, why I was eating and drinking during Ramadan and when I would be back. He interrogated my friend for two hours and tried to rape her. Luckily, she was a strong woman and refused to give in. She managed to persuade him that we couldn't fast, because we were having our periods – a loophole for us – and luckily he went away, but only after ransacking the flat and leaving her with cuts and bruises.

I think he would probably have hurt me badly. He thought I was an unworthy Christian woman breaking the rules of Ramadan. In his eyes, trash like me could be raped and killed. I was also stalked by a taxi driver. When I left the compound in a vehicle, he would suddenly appear behind me. I told my lawyer, who gave me a proper security briefing.

Those incidents filled my mind as I tried to get on with my life in Saudi. With my two younger boys still in the country, I couldn't go anywhere. They were staying with Uncle Adnan, who fortunately was much easier to deal with and gave me bonus hours with them.

This arrangement continued until Christmas 2004. We celebrated the big day itself at Abdullah's house, and because his wife is English we even had a Christmas tree and traditional turkey. We exchanged presents and T's brother picked the boys up at five o'clock because they had school the next day. Here I must make it clear that I had short, constructive chats about my little ones' welfare with Uncle Adnan.

Abdullah and Kathy were due to fly to England the next day, our Boxing Day, to celebrate the New Year. In the evening, I went to their house to deliver some letters, to be posted in England. I'd spoken to Zak on his mobile around five o'clock. He was at a playground with his cousins. We agreed that I'd call him around eight to say goodnight, but when I tried to call him at that time the phone was switched off. I didn't think too much about it, because he could have run out of battery, lost his signal, had an early night or whatever.

At ten o'clock, I received a call from Abdullah, who was at the airport with Kathy waiting for their flight to England. He said, 'Guess who's getting on our flight?'

I knew straight away that my two little boys were leaving

the country. Adnan, obviously under orders from T, had taken them to the airport. A passenger on the plane was detailed to look after them.

Abdullah asked if I had my passport, because he thought I could get a ticket quickly and catch the flight. But it was in a safe at the school and I couldn't get there in time. Abdullah and Kathy kept their heads down and made sure Adnan didn't see them. They boarded the same flight as my boys.

While the plane was in the air, Abdullah managed to make contact with the pilot. He explained to him that on the flight were two children who'd previously been abducted to Saudi Arabia and were now being taken out of the country to England on their own, with no official escort. He told the pilot that this was being done without the knowledge or consent of the mother, who was still in Saudi Arabia.

The pilot contacted Immigration at Heathrow and explained what was going on. When the plane landed, my children were met by Immigration officers and taken away to an office. Abdullah had managed to obtain the number and name of the person who was due to deal with the children. I was able to call this officer myself and provide him with all the details. At first, he was baffled, but he soon made sense of it all.

The Immigration staff got hold of T, who was waiting in the arrivals hall. They told him that they were looking after the children and asked if he'd give his side of the story. The children were handed over to the police and taken to the local station for further delicate questioning.

Immigration gave the police my mobile number and I was later contacted by an officer who was handling my case. 'I'm in a rather difficult position,' he admitted. 'I have your husband here and he's telling me that you're in Saudi Arabia and you're not interested in the children. He says that he's had to arrange to have your children taken to England to be with him and continue their education.'

I was in the middle of teaching a class, on my last day at school, when I received the call. I could see that the tables had turned dramatically.

'You have to believe me,' I pleaded, trying to control a class of five-year-olds at the same time. 'My children have been abducted for a second time. I've been fighting to get my children back for almost three years. I've been to court in Saudi. I can prove all this. You are just going to have to believe me. Please, please, keep the children with you. Do not give them to the father – they could be abducted again. I'm leaving on the next plane out of Saudi.'

The officer must have wondered what he'd done to deserve a case like this. On the one hand, he had a father wanting to collect his children and telling him about their diabolical mother. On the phone, he had a hysterical woman in Saudi Arabia saying the children had been abducted. Not only that, she was speaking from a classroom full of children and her lawyer had arrived on the same plane as the boys.

Before the situation deteriorated any further for the beleaguered policeman, he had a brainwave; he contacted an organisation called Reunite and spoke to its director, Denise Carter. She knew my story inside out and told him it was watertight.

The police took Denise's advice and held on to the children's passports. But they couldn't hold on to the boys any longer; as T and I were still officially a married couple in England and there was no dispute over custody in any British court. T drove off with the boys to his mother's home in Exeter.

My head felt as if it was being crushed by so many bizarre circumstances, all out of my control. Despite my efforts since the abductions, I was on the back foot yet again and struggled to come to terms with the misery of it all. I booked a seat on the next flight, scheduled for 24 hours later.

In the meantime, I ran around collecting outstanding money from my private teaching. I had to leave many of my belongings behind, having packed all that I could, and prepared for the flight, due to leave Jeddah at eleven in the evening. I didn't tell the school I was leaving for good. I said my mother in Denmark was ill and I had to see her. The way things were going, I thought I could easily be back again on the first flight from England. What a nightmare.

I arrived at the airport completely exhausted. I still didn't have possession of my kids, but I thought England would be a much better place to do business with the courts.

When the familiar sight of Heathrow came into view, I pictured my children arriving there, confused, on the previous flight. My friend John from Kent picked me up and drove me to my friend Caroline's house. No, she still wasn't sick of me, despite my constant appearances.

My first task was to call Denise Carter from Reunite. She was thrilled that I'd arrived in one piece and she gave me the name of a solicitor. Between Christmas and New Year wasn't the best time of year to contact the legal profession, so I waited impatiently until 4 January, when practices reopened.

In the meantime, I tried unsuccessfully to contact the

children in Exeter. I had T's phone number and I did get through, but he screamed at me and wouldn't let me talk to them.

I made an appointment to see Ann Thomas, the solicitor recommended by Reunite. I quickly discovered why she had such a good reputation, as she got the ball rolling in a flash. As I told her my story, it was difficult to comprehend that all this had happened to me.

My case went before the High Court in London. I applied for full custody of my children on the grounds of two abductions by their father. My case also stated that the children had expressed their wish to live with their mother. The children were interviewed carefully and gently by Cafcass, the Children and Family Court Advisory and Support Service. The kids wanted to stay with me, but they did want to have some contact with their father. Naturally, I agreed to that.

To protect the children and myself, the court ordered that if T wanted to see them he would have to apply in writing to me. We would both then have to sign an agreement. At the time of writing, he hasn't asked to see the boys.

In just one month, I had interim care and control of the boys. By 17 February 2005, I had full care and control. I rented a house in Sidmouth, on the south Devon coast, and we all moved in. Although the boys were moving school for the umpteenth time in their short lives, now they were settling into a seaside community where love and care abounded.

My youngest son, Adam, found life difficult to start with. Many interests that were second nature to the rest of his classmates were alien to him. One of his new pals asked which football team he supported. Well, he hadn't had access to any sport in Saudi Arabia, so he had to say he didn't know much about football. Not a good answer from a nine-year-old just starting a new school, so his brothers and I helped him find out about teams, to boost his cred.

None of my children knew much about sports because of their background, but I worked hard on this to build their confidence and help them to integrate into the community. They also wanted to change their Arabic names to English names, and I went along with that.

After a year in our new home, the boys were really finding their feet and feeling much more confident. They had friends with whom they shared interests, and enjoyed sleepovers and everything that boys do.

In the summer, we had a wonderful trip to Denmark to see my mother. It was an ideal opportunity to touch base with my family and help the boys to reconnect with their Viking roots.

Yet another move was to follow because the landlord wanted to sell the house we were renting. But I landed on my feet again because, after a long search, I found a delightful town house with a sea view and, at the time of writing, we're still there. It has plenty of room for me and enough space for the kids to chill out.

How I wish T and I had a fairly normal relationship and could share our weekends with the boys. It's never going to happen, because of our years of turmoil. For the record, as I write this, I haven't had a penny in maintenance.

The main players in this unfortunate drama, my four boys, love the Devon countryside. Zak enjoys skateboarding and is currently off on a school trip to France. The twins are doing work experience: Alex feeds the animals on a farm and Max is working in a restaurant.

With four boisterous boys under the same roof, life is far from straightforward. I wasn't prepared when the twins seemed suddenly to become teenagers, with all the issues this brings. I had no run-up to it. I was used to looking after them when they were much younger.

When they first came back from Saudi, their first reaction to a conflict was always to go on the defensive and shout. That's what they'd been used to with their father, and they were younger versions of him. I was having to deal with two boys as tall as me, yelling at each other and fighting. They yelled at me too. It was like a rerun of living with T.

The twins were both overweight, because their Saudi lifestyle had consisted of television, PlayStation, lots of the wrong types of food and no exercise. I knew I had to deal not only with their behavioural problems but also with their diet and exercise. As my nature dictates, I tackled both issues head-on, starting with getting them to eat properly. Crisps, soft drinks and sweets were banned. We didn't have any of those at home, although a small can of cola and a packet of sweets were allowed as a treat if we went out at the weekend. I fed them salads, grilled meat and fish, and anything else that fitted in with their new healthy regime.

Next on the agenda was exercise. I could see they'd missed the boat when it came to sports. They hadn't played rugby, football or cricket. They didn't want to know, so there was no point forcing them. Instead, I found them newspaper rounds and soon they were up at the crack of dawn, riding their bikes around Sidmouth delivering the papers. I also took them running, and the pounds rolled off. They wanted to earn more money, and in no time they were working at the local fish and chip shop.

Sorting out their behaviour was the biggest challenge. I loved having them back, but at the same time I knew I was going to have to curb their aggressiveness. I organised counselling at school, which toned them down a bit. They had to tone down a lot. At mealtimes, one of them would shout, 'Hey, that's mine. Fuck off!' and back would come, 'No, you fuck off, you bastard', as they fought over the last cake. They had no idea how loud they were shouting; they'd lived in a culture where it was the norm, but it wasn't going to happen in my house. After about a year, they were half as noisy. I'm still working on the other half.

Zak has a quieter nature and didn't shout as much as the twins did. Nor was he overweight, so I thought I'd have an easier time with him. There was just one major blot on his copybook and it wasn't his fault. He hated school and he detested homework. I went back in time with him to find the underlying problem. He told me that T used to shout at him and slap him if his homework wasn't up to standard. Zak used to tear sections out of his homework diary to try to avoid more slaps.

I've had problems with Adam too. He has attended so many different schools and didn't seem to make much effort when he started school in Devon. His head teacher complained about his language and behaviour in the playground. Is this my child? I thought. I just couldn't believe what was going on.

As with the other boys, I had to trace what had happened to him, to understand why he was so unruly. By the age of eight, he'd been to six schools. His attitude was: why should

I try so hard, or make friends with the teachers, when I'm not going to stay long? The penny dropped when he told me this was how he felt about school in general.

Adam's behaviour improved when I explained he would be staying at his current school in Sidmouth before going on to college in the same town. Time is the healer in his case. Adam does have some ingrained behavioural issues, but I've been working hard with the school to improve his attitude. Cubs have helped him to mature, and dance classes have boosted his self-confidence. I'm proud to see him perform modern, jazz and street dancing routines.

When we drive up to Southampton to see my friend Caroline and her family, the boys look out at the green hills and fields rolling by. What a contrast with the barren desert that became their home. My children are getting used to living in a free country again.

They don't talk much about what happened. Occasionally, if the subject comes up, they'll discuss it for a while, then one of them will say, 'I don't want to talk about it any more.' That was the hardest part about writing this book: they would go so far, then clam up until the next time the subject was aired. The information came out in dribs and drabs, and inevitably a lot of it was new to me.

So much muddy water has gone under the bridge that all I can say is we're very happy at the moment and England is our permanent home. It's been an extraordinary odyssey and when I look back and read what I've written I'm still stunned by the whole affair.

My main commitment now is to stay here and keep my sons in the same schools. I have no inclination to live in another country; we're staying in Devon, thank you very much.

I would like the boys to grow up into decent human beings, with high morals and respect for themselves and others. And I want us to live happily ever after.

Together.

17

IN MAX'S OWN WORDS

Max decided that I should become a Tesco Mum of the Year. He snuck up to his room and wrote to *Tesco Magazine*. Max's poignant letter topped the Best Children's Entry section. I was so proud of him. Even now, I want to cry as I write this.

Here is what he composed:

'I think my mum is the best. I have a twin brother Alex and two younger brothers, Zak and Adam.

'In 2002, my dad, who is from Saudi Arabia, took us there. It was really hard for us. We'd never been to the country before, it was so different from what we were used to and we didn't speak Arabic. But, worst of all, we had never been apart from our mum before and we really missed her. Mum spent 16 months trying to find out exactly where we were. Then she faced a long, hard battle with the Embassy to get a visa to see us out there.

'When she eventually got to Saudi Arabia she got a job at

an International School so she could be near to us and she fought in the courts to get access to see us. We were allowed to visit her for 24 hours a week.

'It was terrible being away from our mum for so long. But somehow we knew she was doing everything she possibly could to get us back. We love her so much – what she did for us was so brave. And now she helps other mums who are trying to be reunited with their children, giving them hope.'

Max summed up all of my boys' feelings during that terrible, traumatic time, and the people at *Tesco Magazine* knew it was coming straight from the heart. For his contribution to this book, Max put pen to paper again and wrote:

'I remember having lots of fun in Bali. I remember I had plenty of friends, and we used to hang out together.

'To start with, everything was so exciting; Mum and Dad ran their own school, and we all went there. There was a lot of freedom, and we just felt happy all the time. It was hot and we went to the beach. When we didn't go to the beach, we would go to see our friends and swim in their pools.

'All that changed in Saudi. Everything seemed to be hard work. And no one was happy. We thought it was going to be fun in Saudi and that Mum would be coming, but none of that happened. Mum did come, but only because she fought to come to see us.

'If she hadn't made so much effort, we would still be there today, having to speak Arabic, learning the Qur'an and feeling totally miserable. Sometimes I think about how much time I lost in my childhood. When I tell Mum this, she reminds me of the good times we've had, and I just think of those times.

'Now we are in England, we're happy again. It was like a dream come true, and I never thought it would happen so quickly. At first, we were without Mum, but I knew the court people would believe what she was saying, because it was the truth, and they did believe her.

'It is hard for Mum to cope with us, because sometimes we are not very well behaved. When we first came back, we were disruptive and noisy, and I believe Saudi had that effect on us. I'm trying to curb my shouting, and Mum makes sure I know when I've been too loud or aggressive.

'I love England, and would never want to live anywhere else. And, most importantly, I love my mum.'

18

I JUST WANT MY MUM

Remember that Adam was only five years old when he was taken. I've often wondered what he was thinking. Where did he think he was going? What did he feel when he woke up during all those mornings in Saudi Arabia and his mum wasn't there? I didn't get many answers, as he's tried to erase the entire experience from his memory.

To start with, I couldn't get a thing out of him. But gradually he said a little more and I put it together. He went quiet when I asked him about what had happened in Saudi.

I asked him what he would say to his dad if they had a chance to meet up, and his dad offered to wipe the slate clean. What if his father said he'd changed, was sorry and wanted to start again?

'Yeah, right,' he replied ...
'No matter what Dad would say, I know the truth. I have seen it and he can never change. No matter how

245

nice he is ever going to be in the future, I know him and how he treated me.

'Dad hit me on the back of my head when he was doing my homework with me. I was trying hard, but the more he got angry the less I could remember how to do it. I hated it when Dad asked me for my homework diary, and what I had to study the next day. Some of it was in Arabic and it was very hard.

'I got a pain in my stomach when I thought about what I had to do and I couldn't wait til it was over and I could go to sleep. Auntie Alia was good to me. If my dad was shouting or my brothers were teasing me, I said I was tired and went to bed. I just wanted my mum.

'Sorry, I don't want to say any more.'

19

MY MISSION

I never thought I'd end up writing a book about my experiences. For one thing, I would never have known where to start. The idea was hatched shortly after I arrived home from Bali in a mess. My friend Steve, a university professor from Southampton, took me to the David Lloyd leisure club there. He was due to play tennis with one of his friends. I enjoyed watching the match, and afterwards Steve introduced me to his pal.

I discovered that David was a writer, and that Steve had already briefed him on my plight. He was working for the television station Meridian at the time, and said he'd suggest my story to his editor.

The next day, I received a call from the editor and shortly a crew was on its way to see me. I hardly felt nervous during the interview; it all just seemed to come out naturally.

Well, that was only the beginning, of course. The television people kept track of my story and compiled a number of updates. On one occasion, they even sent a television crew to the airport to see me off, and another time they filmed my attempts to obtain a visa.

I remember Richard Spalding and Henry Macaulay from Meridian's newsdesk taking a keen interest, and for that I shall always be grateful. I popped into their offices regularly and they were always keen to hear my news.

They were in repeated contact with the Saudi Embassy press office to ask for comments, and their persistence helped me get my visa. I don't think the Embassy ever told them anything, but at least the Saudis knew there was press interest in my case.

I talked to the Embassy too, of course, so when I first telephoned them they knew all about me. They were usually helpful, but there was little they could do, as my case was so complicated. It took 16 months to move my file from the front desk to the office of His Royal Highness Prince Turki Al-Faisal. But it got there, and I am eternally grateful to him for making my first visit to Saudi Arabia possible. He didn't have to do anything and I imagine he took a risk by his actions.

A news agency saw my story and I started to appear in magazines all over the place. *Woman* and others sent reporters and photographers to report on my plight. Later on, the interest from Tesco sparked another string of articles, including one published by *Take a Break*.

There was no escape from the publicity. Even when I returned to Denmark on holiday, I was approached by a magazine and appeared on the front page.

All this coverage proved to be most helpful in assisting me and hundreds of other women. However, the articles were short and so could only skim the surface. I was pleased to see that some of them mentioned that many other mums were losing their children.

When I came back from Saudi for a short break, I received a call from Steve's friend David, the writer. 'Have you ever thought about writing a book?' he asked. 'It's an astonishing story, topical, and packed with interest.'

I told him that a couple of other people had suggested the same thing.

David said he would act as the ghostwriter. When we started, I was still in the middle of court cases, and I was going backwards and forwards to London. We didn't get much done for several months as I had to sort out my priorities.

I just explained my situation to David. He compiled a structure and, as I told him all about the series of events, he turned it into a dramatic true story, writing beautifully. He didn't change anything; he just converted everything I said into his style. It meant a lot of driving between Devon and Hampshire, where he lives, for us both.

He told me that John Blake Publishing specialised in true stories and mine stood a good chance of making it. We sent off an outline of the book and some pictures.

We didn't hear much for several weeks, but I knew they would be receiving hundreds of submissions. David's phone rang. It was one of Blake's senior editors. 'We'd like to take it on,' she said.

The project has provided therapy for my family. We've gone over what's happened and we've written thousands of words. Now we can concentrate on creating a happier future.

Max is receiving guitar lessons, and he's really into his music. He's also developed into an artist and goes on residential courses in the West Country.

Alex is taking lessons in playing the drums and it's really helping with his development. Of course, I'm dreading the day he arrives home with a drum kit. He's now into tennis too.

Zak has taken up bass guitar and his other great passion is skating. I mentioned earlier that he could easily become a male model. Those looks of his really are something special.

I've already mentioned Adam's dancing, and he has surprised us all with his skill. He takes part in various shows and I'm proud of his efforts. Adam is also a keen cub scout, and he goes off camping with his friends.

This whole episode has affected Adam the most, so I'm happy to see him integrating into the community. I know his experience at a Saudi school, where he didn't understand Arabic but had to join in the lessons, had a negative effect on him. Sometimes he goes very quiet and says nothing for an hour or two. I just leave him alone until he drifts back into his normal zone.

When I look at my children, I can see that they're doing what normal boys do. Maybe they get too excited sometimes, but they're bound to go over the top, considering what they've been through. Whenever they misbehave, I try to work out if it's because of what happened to them, or it's just part of growing up. Sometimes it is one; sometimes the other; sometimes a combination of both.

I feel I had a rough ride, having to cope after the children were abducted. When I got them back, I battled to find housing, schools and everything they needed.

I believe that, as time goes by, my boys' anger is receding and our lives are returning to normal. We're so lucky to have so many people around us who really care, and they're helping us to shape our life as a family.

That call from the publisher was the beginning of a new chapter in my life, and also in the book. And the rest, you know.

Perhaps not quite. Beyond my wish to tell my own story, I believe that women all over the world need to know about the sort of experiences a woman, and especially a mother, can go through in a Muslim society. From this book, they will learn how I fought to get my children back, and, if this makes them demand change in such societies, then my efforts will have been doubly rewarded.

How can it be that the Western world trades with countries such as Saudi Arabia but seems not to be interested in human rights? Certainly, the plight of left-behind parents doesn't get enough recognition. The scenario is all too common nowadays: an Arab man lives in the West, he may not practise his faith, he marries and has children, and when things go wrong he returns to his country of origin with the children. Even though not a devout Muslim, he now uses the protection that his native country offers and makes sure that all ties with the mother are severed. Yes, he can do that and it happens so often.

In my case, during my entire marriage, I never saw my husband pray or go the mosque (apart from the ill-fated visit I mentioned earlier, where I had to find a makeshift scarf to cover my hair). I didn't see him mix with other Saudis or even any Muslims. He lived according to Western values from the age of eight to 48, with one break when he worked for a short time in Saudi Arabia. He swore to me when we got married that it was so horrible there he would never return.

People say to me, 'Helle, you must have known what you were letting yourself in for. If you marry someone from Saudi, surely there's a risk that all this could happen?'

My answer is that I had no way of knowing what would happen. T had lived in England, said he wished to continue with his Western lifestyle and that indeed seemed to be what he wanted.

He also said he despised his religion, so Islam was never a feature of our lives. In fact, my husband was exploring all other religions, so even an outsider at the time would never have predicted the misery I was to face.

Why don't the Saudis, in the name of their religion and compassion, do anything to help all these desperate mothers and children? My youngest son was five years old when he was taken. Under Islamic law, he should have stayed with his mother until the age of nine; however, once the man and the children are in a country such as Saudi Arabia, nothing can be done, and there's no one to help you.

I was lucky to get my children back. The mums that I try to help and support face a brick wall every day. I know that many mothers couldn't contemplate my course of action. I used every trick in every book to be with my kids, and I sailed rather close to the wind at times.

Of all the cases of left-behind mums I've come across, that of my friend Nadia, whose daughter disappeared to Pakistan, is the most tragic. (I tell Nadia's story below, in a separate chapter entitled 'Other Mums, Other Stories'.) Yet, despite death threats and other troubles, Nadia keeps going for the sake of her daughter, Rena. She and so many other women need help urgently. Can't the governments of all those countries which harbour the fathers and the children they have abducted do something to help? Isn't it time that those with the power to do something at least listened?

New websites concerned with abducted children are appearing all the time. One of them claims that there are more than a thousand child abductions by parents every day in the United States. It says there are around two thousand international abductions of American children a year. I assume the compilers did their research, but, whatever the figure, child abduction is now a massive issue all around the world.

Amnesty International says, 'To guarantee the human rights of children is to invest in the future. Children's rights are the building blocks for a solid human rights culture, the basis for securing human rights for future generations.

'As human beings, children are entitled to all the rights guaranteed by the Universal Declaration on Human Rights and the various covenants that have developed from it. But children also need special protection and care. They must be able to depend on the adult world to take care of them, to defend their rights and to help them to develop and realise their potential. Governments pay almost universal lip service to this ideal, yet have signally failed to ensure that the rights of children are respected.'

The European Convention agrees that children should have contact with their parents and with others who have ties to the family, subject to protecting the best interests of the child. Surely most of us believe that, unless there are unusual circumstances – where the child could be at risk, for example – this has to make sense.

Such statements are well intentioned, and it's all very well learning about all these rights for children, but who is there to actually help left-behind women? All these proposals sound wonderful, but in practice your own efforts and luck guide you through. You call up offices everywhere and all they want to do is forget about you and persuade you to go away. Believe me, that's how it is.

Here's another fact to ponder. More often than not, after the kidnapping, the father will do all he can to criticise the mother. In some cases, such as the one involving Nadia, children are made to believe that their mum is dead. Usually, the children are taught to hate their mum, because, they're told, she's such an unworthy person.

Do these governments of Muslim countries believe that hundreds of men had to escape from their evil wives? Again and again, we're called the most horrible names. We're prostitutes, slags, unworthy people, bad mothers and terrible wives. This is relayed to anyone the father meets, not just the children.

So why did they marry us in the first place? Have we all suddenly turned into tarts on street corners? Have we suddenly become unworthy? Do we not love our children? Do these courts in foreign lands really believe that they are dealing with hundreds of good men and hundreds of bad women?

When I sat there, in my heavy gowns in the Saudi court, couldn't they see I was a normal mother who just wanted her children? I believe that some of the officials in the courts could see that maybe, just maybe, I was in the right. But the system did not want to know.

And I suffered the 'unworthy' tag. The boys told me that, from the moment they were taken, I was described as a bad mother, unworthy, a slut and a whore. Even when I arrived in Exeter to pick up some of the children's clothes, T shouted across the street, 'I don't speak to whores.'

Thank God, my sons had the sense to know I was none of those things. They'd had to pretend to hate me, as it was the only way they could avoid going to a horrendous Saudi school. They had no choice in the matter, and their poems and letters from the time tell the real story.

Why did I have to wait 16 months to get into Saudi Arabia? Most mothers whose children have been abducted to that country never manage to get there at all. Luck, as well as my hard work, helped me along the way. Another factor was my Danish background; we Danes are very direct and don't stand any nonsense from anyone. When we talk to people in positions of authority, we talk to them using their first names.

I was brought up to believe that we are all just people, whatever role we play in life. Every time I dealt with someone involved in my case, I sought out the human being behind the official's mask. I never took 'no' for an answer.

So, you see, I was a real pain in the neck. Those people at the Saudi Embassy, hearing my voice for the twentieth time in two days, would have thought, What can we do to appease this woman? I can picture them shaking their heads in despair, wondering how to get rid of me.

Not everyone would have, or could have, gone about it my way. I encountered several mothers who were destroyed by their experiences with officialdom because they are naturally meek and mild people, not used to dealing with aggressive and evasive bureaucrats. They're easily scared off – not their fault – by a harsh voice on the end of a phone.

They couldn't tackle the situation head-on like I did. Well, I suppose I had no choice.

My mission is to spread the truth; help any parent or child affected by abduction; try to persuade anyone who will listen that most mums are normal, loving, law-abiding citizens and not prostitutes. If my book prevents someone, anywhere, from taking a child away from a mother or father, that would be a major achievement for me.

And if my story can spread the word about the growing number of child abductions, at least part of my mission will be accomplished. Sometimes it looks like mission impossible, but left-behind mums are prepared to fight on – to the end.

20

OTHER MUMS, OTHER STORIES
(Names have been changed to protect identities)

When I first set out on my adventure in the desert, I thought I was a lone woman fighting a lonely battle. Although the odds were stacked against me, I went to any lengths to get my children back. I'm one of the few lucky ones.

I've since found out that hundreds of women have faced, and are still facing, my nightmare. I now try to offer support to mums who've had their children taken away and find the pain too much to bear. They just need to talk to someone who's succeeded in being reunited with their children. They need a pep talk and a little hope too.

Some come to visit me. I tell them what happened to me and listen to their situation. If I can give any tips, after going through the mill myself, I gladly do so. Meeting them helps me, because I feel that my experience, although horrid at the time, is being put to good use.

We chat, we go out for a drink, walk along the seafront. I

listen carefully to their haunting stories and keep notes to see if a solution can be found. I discovered that, in my case, I had to try every angle, every trick in the book and even outside the book, to get my children back. I have no regrets about any of it.

Here is a typical story from one of my visiting mums. I've changed her name to Kauser, for obvious reasons. She lives in a little bubble of her own; it should include her ten-year-old son, but it's a bubble that she is forced to inhabit alone.

Kauser has only one reason for living: to find her son, who was snatched in October 2003. So far, she's scoured India, the Middle East and Saudi Arabia. When she arrived at my house, I could sense grief all around her. How much more desperate can a situation get? She's in her mid-forties and suddenly without her only child.

When I first met Kauser, I jumped back in time, to when I was in the same position. As she told me her story, the feeling of helplessness returned; yet this time I was hearing the tragic situation of another person. I felt her pain intensely, maybe because I had been through it all myself.

It is a pain that I can describe like this. You sense that your child is breathing, eating, playing, thinking about you. Yet you are not there to witness any of it. For all you know, the child may think you are dead. You worry that your child is being told bad things about you. Those are some of the elements that make up the pain. I felt it in my stomach, and at times all over my body. It is a pain that comes with intense grief.

Kauser is a dedicated, practising Muslim. She was born in the north of India, married there and came to England with her husband in 1995. She had obtained a PhD in India and lectured there for several years. In England, her husband, Abdul, gained a doctorate.

They had one child, Omar, in 1996. As soon as the child was born, Kauser's relationship with her husband began to deteriorate. Why, you may ask, when a marriage is blessed with a beautiful son? I had, of course, asked myself the same question many times, as I tried to find answers to my own predicament.

Kauser had lived with Abdul for six years before Omar arrived. She recalled that, during those years, her lifestyle had to change. Abdul was very controlling; she had to change her way of life and friends, and even give up her career to please him.

Here's a part of Kauser's story I can't understand, even remotely. If someone does get their head round it, please let me know! While Kauser was pregnant, Abdul said decisions would have to be made, depending on the sex of the child. If a daughter arrived, the mother would be allowed to keep and look after her.

On the other hand, if a boy entered the world, he would have to be given to Abdul's sister, who lived in Libya at that time and later in Saudi Arabia. Perhaps the boy, the inheritor of everything his father owned, including his name, should be brought up in totally traditional surroundings? Maybe that was the thinking behind everything.

Looking back, Kauser believes the whole abduction was planned a long time before it happened. She thought there must have been something wrong with Abdul's mind, because surely not even the most extremes of any religion would allow what he proposed.

Complications developed during the birth of Kauser's

child. After a Caesarean section, she haemorrhaged so badly that she almost died. She was kept in intensive care all night but, as is her nature, battled through.

To Kauser, it was a joy to have a wonderful new addition to her life. Nothing else mattered. Abdul, however, hated the situation because he felt little Omar was getting too much attention. He became even more demanding and controlling.

In Kauser's opinion, her husband tried to destroy her emotionally and physically. Financially, her independence was totally gone. Now she had to make do with basic allowances from Abdul; she dared not ask for anything extra. If she went out for a walk and wanted to get a bus back, she couldn't. She didn't even have the bus fare home.

It was a tough job, giving her child total attention and also meeting Abdul's needs. She decided she had to do everything her husband wanted. Everything and anything. It meant the most appalling hardship, and having to live under the complete control of another person.

The marriage eventually broke down and Abdul moved out. Divorce followed, and Abdul married another woman. They had two children, and for quite a time Abdul seemed to lose interest in Omar. Then he started to have contact again, and took the boy on days out.

Kauser tried several times to tell me how Omar was abducted, but the whole episode was just too painful. She tried so hard, but couldn't find the strength to go over all the details. The memory of the day when her child was taken for an outing with his father to a science park and didn't return is simply too much for her to relate in full.

They still weren't back at three o'clock ... four ... five. At seven, she received a call from Abdul saying Omar was gone and wouldn't be coming back.

She believes Abdul took Omar to India and then Saudi Arabia. Since the day he was taken, she has had no contact whatsoever with her beloved son. She can't find out where he lives or which school he goes to. She knows nothing. As soon as she gets close to finding something out, the boy is taken to another country.

Kauser told me, 'All I care about is how strong he is, how he remembers me and if he is happy. I have to believe, every second of every day, that I will see him again. That is my life.'

I came across a haunting story on an American website, where a broken-hearted mother describes her daily turmoil. It is absolutely spot-on and sums up my former situation perfectly. I have no idea who the woman is, but she speaks for thousands of desperate mothers.

This is what she wrote: 'I am now among the thousands of parents in America and around the world known as "left-behind parents". We are parents who love our children dearly, but who can't see or touch them. We are victims of adults who decided to give themselves instant child custody and get rid of the other parent with no courts involved.

'We are the broken-hearted people who can't pass a playground without feeling a piercing pain in our hearts. Sometimes it gets so bad, that we lock ourselves up in our homes so that we don't run into other children. Our life is now defined in terms of "before the abduction" and "after the abduction". We are not understood, because no one but a parent who has lost a child in this way can understand.

'It is different from losing a child through death because

the pain never ends or begins to fade. We are the parents who can't give up hope because we know that somewhere out there, in a bed across a border far away, is our beloved child without us. We can't grieve the loss, because our child has not died. We don't fit in anywhere else. And we have to hold on to our faith in order to make it through another day!

'Our government, our law-enforcement agencies and judicial bodies, mosques and churches, and our lawyers do not help us. We are told that there is really nothing that can be done and that it is a family matter.

'Our children are held hostage in foreign countries, but they're abandoned and alone at the hands of an adult who did the unthinkable to them. They're not allowed to know their parent. Half of their identity is stripped from them, but no one hears their cry except the left-behind parent.'

Another mum summed up the situation of all betrayed mums when she wrote, 'Child abduction is a parent's worst nightmare. Losing a child for a few minutes on an outing is frightening enough – but imagine returning home where all your children's possessions remain, but the kids are gone.

'Your world collapses. The pain is joined by panic. Emotionally traumatised, parents have to cope with daunting obstacles: finding help, dealing with unfamiliar legal systems, bearing the financial costs of pursuing justice. And they are often misunderstood. Instead of sympathy, they are often faced with disbelieving questions. And the pain never goes away, because the wound cannot be healed.'

Her children weren't taken to Saudi, but to Europe. The two boys were to spend the summer with their father, but never returned to London. She says that, despite the terms of a custody agreement, the boys simply disappeared. Like me, she found that neither the police nor the authorities could offer much help.

She continues, 'If this has been a nightmare for me, imagine what it's like for a child. All children find it difficult to cope with divorce. Children are not only hurt and disappointed; they often feel guilty, believing that they're the source of the family breakdown.

'When a separation leads to abduction, the trauma is that much more severe. Not only do children experience the breakdown of their family, they find themselves wrenched from a loved parent only to realise there is a war between the people they need and love most.'

I'd love to meet these ladies some day. Their stories, their sentiments, are so similar to mine. I count myself so lucky that I have my children back. I pray that, as I write this, they have had some joy in their quest.

Another devastated soul who comes to visit me is Nadia, a British national of Pakistani descent. She's beautiful. When I first met Nadia, I was taken aback by her beauty. She's in her late twenties and looks like one of those supermodels you see on the front of a magazine. She used to work as a model in London before getting married.

Nadia met her future husband, Ahmed, when she was only 16. They met through friends and enjoyed hanging out together. When they married, a year later, the age gap of 12 years didn't seem to be an issue, and the first two years of married life went quite well. The couple had two children: Rena in 1996 and a boy, Zen, in 1998.

Ahmed began to take heroin, a little at first and then

much more. They had argument after argument, and Ahmed started to get into trouble with the law.

Eventually, Nadia could take no more. One day Ahmed was due to go to the Isle of Wight to visit a friend. That was the day she was due to move out, without her husband knowing. She'd arranged to rent a place and was intending to move there with the children.

Ahmed discovered her plan because the estate agent handling the move told him. The estate agent was Asian, so she's not sure whether her plan was leaked deliberately or not. Ahmed went berserk when he found out.

Nadia called the police and told them that she and her children were in danger. She also knew that officers wanted to talk to Ahmed about an unconnected incident, so she told them he was in the house. To this day, Nadia says she's astonished that the police didn't check his details when they came to the couple's home.

Nadia continues in her own words: 'The police arrived, Ahmed had fallen asleep and their radio woke him up. He ran upstairs, had a go at me, realising that I was trying to get away with the two children. I picked my daughter and son up in my arms. He approached me very aggressively, as the police looked on.

'He snatched Rena out of my arms, and out of my grasp where I couldn't reach her. I had my son in my other hand and tried to protect him. Ahmed was screaming and shouting, and trying to take Zen from my arms.

'I was begging the police for help, but they said it was a domestic situation and I needed a solicitor. I explained to the police that I was moving to another address with the children, and he could come and see them there.

'However, because of my situation – which they could see
– I had to get away urgently. Ahmed phoned his family, who
lived locally, and they all turned up at the house.

'I realised that I couldn't get Rena back – there was no
way that Ahmed would let her go – and that Zen was now
a target. I remember I left the house with Zen, who was only
one year old, and he was only half-dressed with no feeder
or anything. I called for a cab and headed for the police
station. Rena was with her father, screaming. My son was
with me, also screaming. What a mess.

'I told my story at the police station and pleaded for
help. They just said I needed to get a solicitor. No change
there, then.

'I ran into a hotel and rang his mum's house, hoping
someone there could help me. I just wanted to explain to his
family that a terrible thing had happened. His mum didn't
want to know.

'I looked through Yellow Pages and called every helpline
I could see. One of them was really helpful. It was a
Saturday, so finding a solicitor and dealing with legal issues
was a problem. They arranged a solicitor for the Monday.

'So I went to Crown Court first thing on Monday morning.
I obtained a residency order for both children, search
warrants and everything in my favour. They served all the
orders that were needed and passed them to the police.

'I gave all sorts of addresses where Ahmed and Rena
might be. The police searched everywhere, and alerted all
ports and airports. They found out that Ahmed had flown to
Pakistan with Rena on the same day as my court hearing. It
had been too late to stop him.

'I was taken in for questioning about what he was wanted

for. I said I'd called them about his alleged offence in the first place, so what more could I do?

'I kept going to the court, but was getting nowhere because the bird had flown. I went to Pakistan myself to search for my daughter.'

Nadia eventually found where her husband and daughter were staying, after six and a half years of detective work. In fact, it was a private detective who traced them to a village in Kashmir. Nadia went to court there to try to obtain custody.

After a protracted legal process costing several thousand pounds, her efforts failed. She was allowed to talk to Rena for several minutes, her first contact since the abduction. The little girl was totally confused. She thought that her mother was dead; that's what she'd been told.

Naturally, Nadia saw her husband as well for the first time since the abduction. He showed no remorse whatsoever. In fact, Nadia said, he didn't appear to have one guilty bone in his body. When she saw him, she felt physically sick.

Ahmed told her that if she didn't drop the court actions she'd have to face the consequences. She knew what that meant. She told him that she had been 'dead' inside for the past six and a half years. As soon as her daughter had gone, much of her life had ebbed away. What remained would stay within her, in her quest to get Rena back.

I shuddered when Nadia told me that she believed her life was in danger. She said the evidence was there and as a result she had changed some of her personal details. Also, she had told the police everything.

At the time of writing, Nadia has her legal papers in order and is preparing to fly to Pakistan once more. My thoughts are with her. And I pray for her every night before I go to sleep.

In some cases, the Hague Convention can help mothers to be reunited with their children. It can help with custody arrangements too. The likes of Albania and Colombia are party to the agreement, but you won't find Saudi Arabia or any Muslim countries on the list.

Countries that are party to the Convention have agreed that 'a child who is habitually resident in one party country, and who has been removed to or retained in another party country in violation of the left-behind parent's custodial rights, shall be promptly returned to the country of habitual residence'. The Convention has also earned a reputation for helping parents to obtain visiting rights abroad.

An abducted child below the age of 16 must be returned, if the application is made within a year of the abduction. There are exceptions, so the small print should be read carefully.

If the application for return is made after a year, the court may use its discretion to decide that the child has become resettled in his or her new country. Yes, there is a chance that the child may not be returned to his or her former home.

Also, a court may refuse to order the return of a child if there is a grave risk that he or she would be exposed to physical or psychological harm. If a child doesn't want to be returned and has reached an age of maturity (this age varies from country to country), that can carry weight too. There are other clauses and conditions that are worth referring to if the convention does happen to cover countries involved in abductions.

All this can come at a hefty price. Even if the countries are party to the convention, single mums and dads can ill afford enormous legal bills. A male friend of mine whose child was taken to Italy now has the child back, but the legal expenses totalled £180,000; that's a lifetime of repayments for most people.

These stories are only the slightest of tips of a gigantic iceberg. I've got to know Nadia and Kauser very well, and I am keen to meet the other two women whose stories I mentioned. Maybe I've become a crusader for what I believe is a totally just cause. Perhaps my experiences, and the court dramas I had to go through, will help another grieving mum. My door is always open.

POSTSCRIPT
AN EXPERT'S VIEW

By Denise Carter, Reunite

I was thrilled to be with Helle when she received her Mum of the Year award from Tesco. We were involved with Helle at an early stage, and her astonishing true story shows what a mum can achieve with determination, persistence and an overpowering desire to be with her children. The problem of child abduction throughout the world is growing at an alarming rate, and I am taking this opportunity to tell you about the work of Reunite and how we work on behalf of left-behind parents, such as Helle.

Reunite is a non-governmental organisation which was formed in 1986 by a group of mothers whose children had been abducted to the United States of America, Algeria and Pakistan. These mothers discovered that there was no organisation in the UK that could help them. After some research, they discovered an organisation in France named the Collectif de Solidarite aux Meres des Enfants Enleves who were working with and helping many

269

French mothers whose children had been abducted to Algeria, Morocco, Turkey and Tunisia.

The British mothers decided to travel to France and join forces with the French women who were undertaking a public demonstration to raise awareness of this growing problem in France. On their return to the UK, these British mothers decided to form an organisation themselves and so Reunite was born. The founder members of Reunite set up meetings with the British government to inform them of what they were intending to do and to see if there were any official figures on the numbers of children who were being abducted from the UK. They also gained the support of a number of Members of Parliament who were also very concerned about this growing problem. Our thanks must go to Sir George Young MP, who provided the corner of his office at the House of Commons so an advice line could be established to provide advice, information and support to members of the public who were subject to the abduction of children and those parents who feared abduction.

In 1990, Reunite was instrumental in the formation of the All Party Parliamentary Group on Child Abduction, which was chaired by Ian McCartney MP, and through the work of this group we saw international parental child abduction placed firmly on the British political agenda. The same year, we received charitable status and moved to larger premises in West London. Government funding was secured from the then Lord Chancellor's Department (now known as the Department for Constitutional Affairs), the Foreign and Commonwealth Office and the Home Office.

In 1993, Reunite evolved from a parent-support network to an information and resource centre covering abduction to and from the UK, prevention of abduction, and assisting parents who were trying to maintain contact across international borders.

Cases of international parental child abduction are split into two categories. The first category is abduction to those countries that are members of the 1980 Hague Convention on the Civil Aspects of International Child Abduction, to which there are 74 Member States. The Convention looks at returning a child to the country of habitual residence so that country can make any decisions in the best interests of the child. For further information on the Hague Convention, please contact the International Child Abduction and Contact Unit, website www.offsol.demon.co.uk (and follow the prompt to international functions), or the website of the Permanent Bureau of the Hague Convention on Private International Law: www.hcch.net.

All other countries are classed as Non-Hague States; if an abduction occurs to one of these countries, then the parents would have to apply through the domestic courts of these countries for the return of the children. Reunite has completed a research project into many of these States' laws and practices, and the information is available through the Reunite advice line.

Reunite is now in its twentieth year and the advice line remains the heart of the organisation. All projects and work that we undertake are linked to the needs of the parents who contact us. The advice line also provides advice and information to lawyers, police and other professionals working in this specialist field.

On average, the advice line takes over five thousand calls each year and sadly the number of cases reported to us continues to grow. The reasons for abduction vary; often there is a power and control element, religious and cultural differences, or the fact that the marriage has broken down and both parents believe that the interests of the children are best served by the children living with them as the primary carer.

Reunite works in the best interests of the child, and has completed groundbreaking research into the effects of abduction on the children by hearing their voice as well as that of their parents. This report can be viewed or obtained by contacting the Reunite office.

I would like to thank Helle for giving me the opportunity to raise awareness of the work of Reunite. We were able to help her be reunited with her beautiful children in January 2005, and I had the opportunity earlier this year to meet Helle and the boys when I was asked to present her with the award from Tesco. On meeting Helle, it confirmed to me the strength of character she has, and the love that she and the boys have for each other. It was also very clear that the boys are happy and have settled back into their lives in the UK.

I hope that this remarkable account of Helle's fight to be reunited with her children is an inspiration to all those parents who find themselves in a similar position and that it gives them the strength to keep working and fighting for the return of their children.

Helle, I wish you and the boys a peaceful and positive life together. You are really an inspiration to us all.

Denise Carter OBE,
Director
Reunite International Child Abduction Centre
P.O. Box 7124
Leicester, LE1 7GA

For further information on the work of Reunite, please view our website (www.reunite.org) or contact the Reunite advice line on 0044 (0) 116 2556 234.